STATE OF MAINE

F. William Messier   )

David E Robinson   )
)
MAINE REPUBLIC FREE STATE   )

David E Robinson   )

     Plaintiffs   )
)
     v.   )
)
THE INTERNAL REVENUE   )

Douglas H. Shulman   )
)
INTERNAL REVENUE SERVICE   )

Manual Dias Saldana   )

Joline P. Hendershot   )

Jason S. Rogers   )

Patrick Frie   )
)

MAINE SUPERIOR COURT

752 High Street

Bath, ME 04530

Docket No. BATSC-CV-2012-00036

COMPLAINT

AND

MOTION FOR SUMMARY JUDGEMENT

OR

JURY TRIAL

UNITED STATES SENATE
Senator Susan M. Collins

T-MOBILE USA INC
Chief Financial Officer

UNITED STATES CELLULAR
Chief Financial Officer

CROWN ATLANTIC COMPANY
Chief Financial Officer

SPRINT UNITED MGMT COMPANY
Chief Financial Officer

ATT&T MOBILITY LLC
Chief Financial Officer

ATLANTIC COAST RADIO LLC
Chief Financial Officer

TOWN OF BRUNSWICK
Chief Financial Officer

MAINE RSA 1 INC
Chief Financial Officer

NEXTEL COMMUNICATIONS
Chief Financial Officer

CRITICAL ALERT SYSTEMS LLC
Chief Financial Officer

AT&T WIRELESS SERVICES INC
Chief Financial Officer

ACTIVE COMMUNICATIONS
Chief Financial Officer

RADIO COMMUNCATION MGMT INC
Chief Financial Officer

                                       Defendants

PLAINTIFFS

F. William Messier
40 Tower Lane
Brunswick, ME 04011

David E Robinson
3 Linnell Circle
Brunswick, Maine 04011

MAINE REPUBLIC FREE STATE
David E Robinson, A.G.
3 Linnell Circle
Brunswick, Maine 04011

DEFENDANTS

THE INTERNAL REVENUE
Douglas H. Shulman, Comm.
10th & Penn. Ave NW
Washington, DC 20004

INTERNAL REVENUE SERVICE
Manual Dias Saldana, Secretary
P.O. Box 4515
San Yuan, Puerto Rico 00902

Jason S. Rogers, Special Agent
Patrick Frie, Agent
220 Maine Mall Road
South Portland, ME 04106

Joline P. Hendershot, Agent
217 Main Street
Lewiston, ME 04240

UNITED STATES SENATE
Susan M. Collins, Senator
One Canal Plaza, Suite 802
Portland, Maine 04101

T-MOBILE USE INC
12920 SE 38TH STREET
BELLEFUE WA 98006

UNITED STATES CELLULAR
8410 WEST BRYN MAWR #700
CHICAGO IL 60631

CROWN ATLANTIC COMPANY
2000 CORPORATE DRIVE
CANNONSBURG PA 15317

SPRINT UNITED MGMT CO.
12502 SUNRISE VALLEY DRIVE
RESTON VA 20191

ATT&T MOBILITY LLC
909 CHESTNUT STREET
ST LOUIS MO 63101

ATLANTIC COAST RADIO LLC
779 WARREN AVE
PORTLAND ME 04103

TOWN OF BRUNSWICK
28 FEDERAL STREET
BRUNSWICK ME 04011

MAINE RSA 1 INC
100 CUMBERLAND BLVD 900
ATLANTA GA 30339

NEXTEL COMMUNICATIONS
201 RT 17N 12TH FLR
RUTHERFORD NJ 07070

CRITICAL ALERT SYSTEMS LLC
100 LARRABEE ROAD STE 150
WESTBROOK ME 04092

AT&T WIRELESS SERVICES INC
16331 NE 72ND WAY
REDMOND WA 98052

ACTIVE COMMUNICATIONS
12 FIRST STREET STE 5
TOPSHAM ME 04086

RADIO COMMUNICATIONS MGMT
158 RAND ROAD
PORTLAND ME 04102

NOW COME Plaintiffs F. William Messier and David E. Robinson who state as follows:

COMPLAINT
CONSPIRACY TO COMMIT FRAUD
UNLAWFUL SEIZURE OF PRIVATE PERSONAL PROPERTY
FRAUDULENTLY MISLEADING THIRD PARTY PAYORS
MULTIPLE VIOLATIONS OF THE U.S. FAIR DEBT COLLECTION PRACTICES ACT
TREASON AGAINST THE UNITED STATES REPUBLIC AND THE PEOPLE OF THE UNITED STATES

RELIEF REQUESTED

Accordingly, the Plaintiffs hereby request that this Honorable Court:

1. Declare the IRS in violation of 15 USC Chapter 41, Subchapter V - DEBT COLLECTION PRACTICES.

2. Order the IRS to cease and desist violating 15 USC Chapter 41, Subchapter V - DEBT COLLECTION PRACTICES.

3. Order Messier's (15) Payors to cease and desist sending Messier's payments to the IRS.

4. Order Messier's (15) Payors to submit to the Court a total accounting of the funds that each one has surrendered to the IRS in this regard.

5. Order the IRS to refund and pay twice the amount of the payments surrendered to the IRS by Messier's Payors directly to Messier within 20 days.

5. Order the Office of Maine Senator Susan M. Collins to announce the settlement of this case in the House of Representatives in Maine and Washington, DC.

6. Grant such other and further relief as the Court deems proper and just.

Dated at Brunswick, Maine this 25th day of September 2012.

DAVID E. ROBINSON
Interim Attorney General for the
Maine Free State Trust

COUNT I
Unlicensed Practice

COUNT II
Failure to Disclose Material Facts

COUNT III
Misrepresentation of Terms and Conditions

COUNT IV
False or Misleading Advertising

COUNT V
Exploitation of Vulnerable Individuals

COUNT VI
Failure to Refund Funds

COUNT VII
Deprivation of Remedies under the Law

Attested to and signed under the penalty of perjury in Cumberland County, Brunswick, Maine, September, 25, 2012

F. William Messer, agent

David E Robinson, agent

CONTENTS

INTRODUCTION

This is an action under the
United States Fair Debt Collection Practices Act
15 USC Chapter 14 Subchapter V - Debt Collection
and a Motion for Summary Judgment or Jury Trial
Designed for Summary Judgment
so that no one person has to side in judgment
either for nor against the IRS.
May the Truth Stand and Testify for Itself.

PREFACE

COMMERCE consists of a mode of interacting and resolving disputes whereby all matters are executed under oath by sworn affidavit executed under the penalty of perjury as true, correct, and complete.

An affidavit is one's solemn expression of his truth. When you issue an affidavit you get the power of an affidavit. You also incur the liability involved.

An unrebutted affidavit becomes judgment in commerce. Proceedings consist of contests of commercial affidavits wherein the unrebutted points in the end stand as truth to which judgment of law applies.

Commercial Law is pre-judicial and non-judical.

A claim can be satisfied only through (1) rebuttal by affidavit point by point; (2) resolution by jury; or (3) payment or performance of the claim.

The conflict between Commercial Affidavits gives a clean basis for resolving disputes.

Please Note
Treasury Order 150-10 delegates authority to the Commissioner of THE INTERNAL REVENUE to administer the Internal Revenue Code, but makes no mention of the INTERNAL REVENUE SERVICE.

The INTERNAL REVENUE SERVICE is a private, non federal debt collection agency for the for the private, non federal Federal Reserve Bank.

Revenue Agents operating in all the states are not United States employees. IRS agents and clerks do not have to pay income taxes.

(26 USC Subtitle F, Chap. 64, Subchap. D Part II, Section 6331(a))

The only people required to pay income taxes are "persons in the civil, military, naval, or other employment service of the United States, including Senators and Representative and delegates in Congress."

Postal clerks are paid by the Secretary of the Treasury of the United States. IRS agents are paid by Secretary of the Treasury of Puerto Rico.

From the US FDCPA

Section 805(b) Communication with Third Parties:

"Without the prior consent of the consumer a debt collector may not communicate with any person other than a consumer, etc."

Section 807(1) False or misleading representations:

"A debt collector may not use any false, deceptive or mis-leading representation or means in connection with the collection of any debt."

"...may not give the false implication that the debt collector is affiliated with the United States..."

"...may not give the false representation of the character of any debt..."

F. WILLIAM MESSIER

F. William Messier (hereafter "Messier") owns the highest piece of real estate in Brunswick, Maine (Cumberland County) on which (6) telecommunication towers are placed, (4) of which serve (15) paying customers (hereafter "Payors").

The Defendants are stealing Messier's contracted lease receipts via his (15) Payors and violating his right to due process of law — and they refuse to respond to his lawful demands.

Sometime around the beginning of 2012, Bill received a letter from an IRS agent asking him to come to the IRS office in South Portland Maine for a meeting concerning income taxes that they claim are due and payable to the IRS.

Messier responded to the request with a letter of his own stating that he had no reason to believe that he was under the jurisdiction of the IRS because he was not an <u>officer</u>, <u>agent</u>, nor an <u>employee</u> of the corporate United States.

Later, Messier began to receive copies of **NOTICES OF LEVY** that IRS agent Joline P. Hendershot (hereafter "Hendershot") was sending to each of his fifteen lease customers demanding that their company Payor send Messier's lease payment to her instead — and the Payors have been doing so ever since.

Messier objected to the IRS seizure of funds that were lawfully due him, and notified IRS agent Hendershot and his lease payment Payors to that effect — many times by postal mail to no avail.

Messier has received many copies of fraudulent **NOTICES OF LEVY** (Forms 668-A) that Hendershot has been sending to his customers that carry only a stamped signature (or no signature at all) which claim that an IRS agent has been assigned to examine alleged tax returns of his, and that he owes income taxes for several years, that he has not paid.

The Defendants are proceeding on the false assumption that Messier has an obligation of income tax liability to them or the **IRS debt collection agency** of and for the private for profit non-federal Federal Reserve Bank.

Messier gave each of the IRS Defendants NOTICE of those errors and declared his objection to all such presumed claims by them or anyone else in the IRS, i.e. Messier denies that he has any obligation of income tax liability to them or the IRS.

It is Messier's intention to obey all laws that legitimately impose any requirement or obligation upon him.

But he has no intention to volunteer where no obligation exists, especially when a waiver of his rights is involved. He is relying on among other things what the Supreme Court held long ago:

> "An individual may be under no obligation to do a particular thing, and his failure to act creates no liability; but if he voluntarily attempts to act and do a particular thing, he comes under an implied obligation in respect to the manner in which he does it." — *Guardian T&D Co. v. Fisher (1906) 26 S.Ct. 186,188.*

Therefore, Messier has determined that he is not subject to the defendants nor the IRS. Neither is he one to whom they can demand that he produce personal documents and records for their review, or that he has any obligation to submit those records for an examination by them, or others, for any purpose.

Messier is being financially damaged by the loss of his overhead capital amounting to well more than $60-$80,000.00 dollars over the past six to eight months.

Complaint and Motion for Summary Judgement or Jury Trial

TESTIMONY

BASIS OF CLAIM

The IRS is a Private Debt Collection Agency that has NO authority to TAKE by Force any records, property, money, or thing of value **without a Court Order from a United States District Court**.

Citizens do not have to respond to requests for documents, nor orders to produce documents, nor summonses from the **IRS Collection Agency;** that are **not issued under Court Order**.

This ruling applies also to third party agencies and persons; and includes all administrative orders and directives. — *see Schultz v. IRS, U.S. Court of Appeals, 2nd Circuit, Washington, DC, Case No. 04-0196-cv.*

Subsequent actions to enforce this ruling have been made by the 2nd Circuit Court.

The second ruling by the Court of Appeals on motion by the IRS for Relief is substantially stronger in Court Ruling clarifications and details.

The IRS "Takes the position", however, that they can disregard Court Rulings in one Circuit, and continue operations as usual, and issue false documents in any other Circuit, and issue Subpoenas, Liens, Summonses, Levys, Notices of Levy, Letters of Demand for Records, and assess civil fines (illegally on their own issue) without due process of law or a hearing of any kind.

Any Court Ruling in the favor of the IRS is wrongly deemed to apply *everywhere.* See IRS Publication." — *"Your Federal Income Tax for Individuals".*

Supreme Court Citations referenced in the *Schultz v. IRS* — supporting Schultz:

- *The Antelope,* 23 U.S. 66, 120 (1825)

- *Citizens Savings & Loan Assn v. City of Topeka,* 87 U.S. 655 (1874)

- *Butchers' Union Co. v. Crescent City Co.,* 111 U.S. 746 (1884)

- *Adair v. United States,* 208 U.S. 172

- *Flint v. Stone Tracy Co.,* 220 U.S. 107 (1911)

- *Stratton's Independence Ltd. v. Howbert,* 231 U.S. 399, 414 (1913)

- *Brushaber v. Union Pacific RR Co.,* 240 U.S. 1 (1916)

- *Peck v. Lowe,* 247 U.S. 165

- *Doyle v. Mitchell Bros. Co.,* 247 U.S. 179 (1918)

- *Eisner v. Macomber,* 252 U.S. 189 (1920)

- *Truax v. Corrigan,* 257 U.S. 312, 331, 338 (1921)

- *Bowers v. Kerbaugh-Empire Co.,* 271 U.S. 174D (1926)

- *Tyler v. U.S.,* 281 U.S. 497, at 502

- *Railroad Retirement Board v. Alton Railroad Co.,* 295 U.S. 330, 55 S. Ct 758 (1935)

- *Murdock v. Pennsylvania,* 319 U.S. 105 at 113 (1943)

- *James v. United States,* 366 U.S. 213, p.213, 6L Ed 2nd 246 (1961)

- *Central Illinois Public Service Co. v. United States,* 435 U.S. 21 (1978)

FRAUDULENT USE OF NOTICE OF LEVY
Form 668-A

Most IRS agents have been mentally programmed to be aggressive in dealing with sovereign citizens, and because we have allowed them to do anything short of murder, they often ignore legal procedures and responsibilities which are written up in their own Internal Revenue Codes.

The use of Form 668-A, Notice of Levy is an example of the fraudulent use of instruments and the usurping of powers not available to them.

Please turn to the back side of the Notice of Levy and read the first paragraph.

You will notice that it begins with the header: EXCERPTS FROM THE INTERNAL REVENUE CODE

Sec. 6331. Levy and Distraint

(b) Seizure and Sale of Property

Why does this legal document begin with paragraph (b)? Where is paragraph (a), the most important paragraph? Obviously we don't have the entire contract.

Are they trying to hide something from us? Section 6331(a) in the Internal Revenue Code has nothing to do with us.

All these years the IRS has been using the wrong instrument on us.

Section 6331(a) reads as follows:

(a) Authority of Secretary [of the Treasury].

If any person liable to pay any tax neglects or refuses to pay the same within 10 days after notice and demand, it shall be lawful for the Secretary to collect such tax (and such further sum as shall be sufficient to cover the expenses of the levy) by levy upon all property and rights to property (except such property as is exempt under section 6334) belonging to such person

or on which there is a lien provided in this chapter for the payment of such tax.

Levy may be made upon the accrued salary or wages of any officer, employee, or elected official of the United States, the District of Columbia, or any agency of instrumentality of the United States or the District of Columbia, by serving notice of levy on the employer (as defined in section 3401 (d)) of such officer, employee, or elected official.

If the Secretary makes a finding that the collection of such tax is in jeopardy, notice and demand for immediate payment of such tax may be made by the Secretary and, upon failure or refusal to pay such tax, collection thereof by levy shall be lawful without regard to the 10-day period provided in this section.

The application of the authority to collect a tax by levy is strictly limited by the very important words in the beginning of section 633l(a).

The words, "If any person liable to pay..." describe those "persons" (individuals, trusts, estates, partnerships, associations, companies, or corporations) to whom the section applies.

If a "person" is not liable for a tax, that "person" cannot be liable to pay it, so it is easy to see that the application of the power of levy under section 6331 is limited to those "persons" that are liable for a tax.

Court decisions, for example ***Botta v. Scanlon,*** 288F.2d504,(1961), and authoritative books on law, such as Sutherland's Rules of Statutory Construction (sec.66.01 and 66.03), clearly state that **the only way that an individual can become liable for a tax is by legislative action** (a statue of IR Code section.)

Therefore, the only "persons" against whom a levy under **IR Code section 6331** can be legally be made are those upon whom liability for a tax is imposed **by some section of the IR Code.**

There is no section making any citizen liable for payment of income tax on his own behalf.

In fact, we have tried to find the law that requires a citizen to file a 1040 Form.

We have asked California's Mel Levine, Member of United States Congress, and Senator Daniel Inouye (D, Hawaii) who in turn asked the Congressional Research Service.

They report that they have abandoned the search for such law.

Others have come to the same conclusion. Even the Supreme Court.

So, the power of levy in section 6331 could not legally be applied against Messier.

Note that Section 6331 states that it is lawful for the <u>Secretary</u> (IRS by delegation) **to collect tax by means of a levy after notice** [of assessment] **and demand** [for payment] **has been sent to the person liable.**

The date and circumstances when a levy occurs are defined very clearly in Section 6502 (b) and 6335 (a).

Section 6502 (b) Date When Levy in Considered Made.
The date on which a levy on property or rights to property is made shall be **the date on which the notice of seizure provided in section 6335 (a) is given.**

Section 6335 Sale of Seized Property.
(a) As soon as practicable after seizure of property, notice in writing shall be given by the Secretary to the owner of the property...

Section 333.1 of the IRS Legal Reference Guide for Revenue Officers (I 0-29-79) explains that **a levy cannot occur without first a seizure.**

"Whether a levy, or notice of levy, is the administrative method employed to collect delinquent taxes, it should be borne in mind that **a levy requires that the property levied upon be brought into legal custody of the United States government through seizure.**

There must be actual or constructive physical appropriation of the property levied upon.

Mere intent to reduce to possession and control is insufficient."

Under 7608(b), only criminal investigators (special agents) **are authorized to conduct seizures.** There is no statutory provision authorizing criminal investigators to delegate their authority to others.

Therefore, there can be no levy until there has been a seizure of targeted property, putting it in the possession of the government.

If there has been no seizure, there can be no legitimate notice of seizure.

Since a levy cannot occur until the date on which a legitimate notice of seizure is sent, **the IRS has no authority to levy on any property that is not in the possession of the U.S. Government.**

Note that the items subject to seizure under the **IR Code** are very limited and are related to the excise taxes imposed by Subtitles D and E of the **IR Code.**

They are defined in **Sections 7321 & 7608(b)(2)(c)** as "<u>property subject to forfeiture</u>".

They are defined as "Any property on which ... any tax is imposed by this title..." (e.g., **distilled spirits, tobacco products, etc. listed in Code Subtitles D and E**).

Property such as bank accounts, automobiles, homes, businesses, buildings and other assets belonging to individuals are not subject to seizure under the IR Codes **unless they are involved in activities related to <u>taxable commodities</u> on which taxes are not paid.**

Under no circumstances can such property be lawfully seized for income tax **without an attachment order from a court of law.**

Notice that Section 6331(a) creates the power to levy; "upon the accrued salary or wages of any <u>officer</u>, <u>employee</u>, or <u>elected official</u> of the United States, the District of Columbia, or any agency of instrumentality of the United States or the District of Columbia." **because those monies are already in the possession of the Government,** so no court order is needed to force the surrender of the money.

But a court order is needed to compel surrender of money by third parties such as banks.

A notice of Levy form has no force of law to compel anyone to surrender property to the IRS.

The IRS's power of levy differs from the power of levy of a sheriff acting under the authority of a court order.

Using a court order, the Sheriff can levy (take possession of for the purpose of sale) any property subject to the court order.

But the IRS, being only an administrative agency in the executive branch of government, has No judicial powers to authorize the seizing of what ever property it chooses.

As evidenced by the provisions of 633l(a) and 6502(b), **levy may be made upon property which is already in the possession of the government.** Their limitation is pointed out in IRC **Section 7401**.

Section 7401. AUTHORIZATION

No civil action for the collection or recovery of taxes, or of any fine, penalty, or forfeiture, shall be commenced **unless the Secretary** [of the Treasury of Puerto Rico] **authorizes or sanctions the proceedings and the Attorney General of the "taxpayers" state or his delegate** [court order] **directs that the action be commenced.**

Section 7403 of the IR Code requires the government to file suit in federal district court against the person from whom they are trying to collect. It also requires that all persons claiming any interest in the property that IRS wants to attach, must be served with papers notifying them of the law suit.

Only after a hearing (due process of law) on the suit where a judgment is rendered in favor of the government by a court of law, can a lawful attachment order be issued.

If there has been no hearing by a court of law **(tax court is not a court of law),** there can be no lawful attachment, and there can be no compulsion whatsoever for any one to surrender any property to the IRS as a result of a fraudulently delivered **"Notice of Levy."**

If you as a Payor rely upon the illegal use of **Form 668-A** to send money to the IRS, **without an accompanying court order, you will be named as a party to fraud.**

Fraud is defined in Blacks Law Dictionary as follows:

An intentional perversion of truth for the purpose of inducing another in reliance upon it to part with some valuable thing belonging to him or to surrender a legal right; a false representation of a matter of fact, whether by word or by conduct, by false or misleading allegation, or by concealment of that which should have been disclosed, which deceives and is intended to deceive another so that he shall act upon it to his legal injury.

The consequences of fraud, according to the United States Supreme Court, are as follows:

Fraud destroys the validity of everything into which it enters. — *Nudd v. Burrows*

Fraud vitiates everything. — *Boyce v. Grundy*

Fraud vitiates the most solemn contracts, documents, and even judgments. — *U.S. v. Throckmorton*

The Following stipulations stand as truth under the Commercial law of the Uniform Commercial Code (UCC) because they were not rebutted point for point under the penalty of perjury by Defendants, Hendershot, Rogers, and Frie.

1 • There is no law that requires most Americans to file an individual tax return.

2 • The Internal Revenue Service (IRS) wasn't created by an act of Congress.

3 • The Public Salary Tax Act (26 USC 1) was passed in 1930 to impose a tax upon the income of federal employees, U.S. citizens [of the District of Columbia] and non-resident aliens.

4 • The Public Salary Tax Act of 1939 did Not apply to Citizens of the forty-eight (48) now fifty (50) States.

5 • Congress passed the Victory Tax Act of 1942, after Pearl Harbor was bombed by Japan on December 7, 1941 to raise money to support an Army, in accordance with Article I, Section 8, Clause 12 of the Constitution of the United States of America:

6 • Article I, Section 8, Clause 12 states that "Congress shall have Power ... To raise and support Armies, but no Appropriation of Money to that Use shall be for a longer term than two Years."

7 • IRS 1040 Forms only apply to government employees, citizens and residents of the District of Columbia, and non resident aliens.

8 • The Bureau of Internal Revenue sent out 1040 Forms in 1942 to the general public in the forty-eight states, even though the Victory Tax Act of 1942 didn't apply to the general public in the forty-eight states.

9 • Most people voluntarily filed a Form 1040 in 1942, 1943, and in 1944 not realizing that direct taxes were not allowed according to the U.S. Constitution and that the Victory Tax Act of 1942 was an extension of the Public Salary Tax Act of 1939 which referred to the public salaries of public government employees and not the general public.

10 • Congress repealed the Victory Tax Act of 1942 on May 29, 1944 but the news media did not publicize the repeal.

11 • The Bureau of Internal Revenue mass mailed 1040 Forms to the general public in 1945 just to see what would happen. (a scheme)

12 • The public filled out the 1040 Forms and mailed them in along with their checks mistakenly thinking that the Victory Tax Act was mandatory in the then forty-eight (48) States without knowing that the Act had been repealed.

13 • The Bureau of Internal Revenue has continued the Fraud on the Citizens of the forty-eight (48) now (50) States and has continued to fraudulently send out Form 1040's each and every year ever since.

14 • The mainstream media are accessories after the fact to the IRS Fraud.

15 • The name of the "Public Salary Tax Act of 1939" was changed to the "Internal Revenue Code" (IRC) and amended in 1953 and 1987.

16 • The "Internal Revenue Code" (IRC) only applies to the District of Columbia and the federal territories and possessions.

17 • There is no authority for the IRS to operate within the fifty (50) states of the Union.

18 • The Internal Revenue Bureau (IRB) and the Internal Revenue Service (IRS) were not created by an act of Congress.

19 • The Internal Revenue Bureau (IRB) and the Internal Revenue Service (IRS) are Not agencies of the Department of the Treasury of the United States.

20 • The Internal Revenue Bureau (IRB) and the Internal Revenue Service (IRS) are agencies of the Department of the Treasury of Puerto Rico.

21 • All Revenue Agents and Officers work as employees for the Department of the Treasury of the Commonwealth of Puerto Rico.

22 • The Internal Revenue Service does not have any jurisdiction or authority over a Sovereign Citizen nor Union State to enforce the unlawful provisions of the Internal Revenue Code.

23 • The "Internal Revenue Service" has no legal jurisdiction in any of the fifty (50) States of the Union of American States.

24 • The IRS is perpetrating the greatest income tax fraud on the Citizens of America that this country has ever ignorantly not seen. (no license)

25 • The IRS deals with a person's fictional strawman under Administrative law according to Title 26

26 • The IRS is a debt collection agency for the non-federal Federal Reserve Bank and operates under Title 15 instead of Title 26.

27 • Title 15 comes under the FAIR DEBT COLLECTIONS PRACTICES ACT (FDCPA) and deals with natural persons who have human and constitutional rights under Private law.

28 • The IRS is a private for-profit debt collection agency for the non-federal Federal Reserve Bank.

29 • The IRS is a private for profit debt collection agency under Legislative branch of the government which is Private law.

30 • When dealing with the IRS under Title 15 a person is seen to be a natural person who can invoke the private protections and rights of Constitutional law.

31 • The Accused are acting under wrongfully assumed Authority and Powers and under the pretense and color of office, laws and title.

32 • The Accused have been given due Notice of Messier's ownership of real and personal property stolen, embezzled, converted and/or purloined, by and through certain illegal and unlawful successive acts including but not limited to wrongful issuance of 20 or more NOTICES OF LEVY issued by JOLINE P. HENDERSHOT between April 15, 2012 and today that are effecting the false impression of actual levies warranted by a judge.

33 • The above claim 32 was effected by out of court procedures and modes under the appearance of legitimacy to coerce fifteen (15) or more customers of FRANCIS WILLIAM MESSIER into illegally and unlawfully seizing, stealing, retaining and being in unlawful possession, custody and/or control of approximately $80,000.00 "Dollars" so far which was/is lawfully payable to Francis William Messier domiciled on the land at 40 Tower Lane, near Brunswick, Maine 04011, in the County of Cumberland, within the territorial jurisdiction of the Republic of Maine.

34 • The Accused and their corporate Officers, Employer, Agents and/or Representatives are "agents of a foreign Principal" pursuant to 22 USCS 611.

35 • The Accused and their Officers, Employer, Agents and/or Representatives are directed, controlled, financed, subsidized and/or compensated for aiding, abetting, counseling, commanding, representing, and procuring the gathering of information, soliciting, collecting, disbursing, dispensing money, currency, or other things of value for or in interest of (A) "The United Nations" whose seat of government is in New York City, New York (22 USCS 287, 61 Stat. 3416); (B) "The Association" (22 USCS 284 et seq.); (C) "The Bank" and (D) "The Fund" (22 USCS 286 et seq.); and their subsidiary artificial beings pursuant to Public Law 94-564, Public Law 86-147, Public Law 89-369, Public Law 93-83, 87 Stat. 197, et cetera. (See also: 22 USCS 263(a); 22 USCS 285(g); 22 U.S.C.S. 287(j); 26 USCS 6103(k)(4); Executive Order 10033.) (Whew!)

36 • Internal Revenue Service Agents are in fact engaged in inter-agency, international stipulations, agreements and commerce with "The Association"

and/or the "International Bank for Reconstruction And Development" and its many-faceted subsidiary, artificial beings, pursuant to "Treasury Delegation Order No. 91 (Rev. 1)," and "Service Agreements described in paragraph IV, of the General Agreement between the Treasury Department and the Agency for International Development, dated February 14, 1966" (Bretton Woods Agreement; 22 U.S.C.S. 284 et seq.).

37 • The character of "The Association," "The Bank," "The Fund," and the Governor of the Fund (Secretary of the Treasury) (See: 22 USCS 286(a)), his associates, delegates, officers, employees, representatives, servants, and/or agents, being the real parties in interest, were and are now subject to Article III, Section 2, Clauses 1 and 2, as a matter of supreme Law, and/or Act of Congress, 22 USCS 286(g).

38 • The acts of the Accused and/or authorization of acts are acts committed under Letters of Marque issued on behalf of Their Foreign Principal and its artificial Organizations, and clearly in excess of the express and conditional, delegated and vested Powers and Authority, as established by the Ordained Constitution for the Union of several States of the United States of America.

39 • Francis W. Messier has RIGHTFULLY DEMANDED the immediate return of the above stated sum pursuant to 18 USCS 645, and all other property and rights to property as stolen, confiscated and expropriated in violation of Act of Congress, coded Title 18 USCS 654 and 241; and under authority of the Declaration of Independence; the Ordained Constitution for the united States of America (1787), Article I Section 10, Clause I; Act of Congress, coded Title 31 USCS 314, 321, 5112; Public Law 93-110, Article IV, Section 2; and Amendments I, IV, V, VI, IX, and X.

40 • Francis W. Messier has RIGHTFULLY DEMANDED the same said property be returned to his personal care, custody, possession and control, to the address given above from which it was taken, seized, stolen and confiscated by his customers under the fraudulent orders of the Accused.

41 • Due to the residency and collateral fact that the Accused and/or their Foreign Principals, Organizations, Associations, Officers, Employees, Representatives, Servants, or other Individuals acting under their direction and control, are incapable of maintaining the integrity of the de jure, lawful, Constitutional Monetary System of the de jure Union of several Republican States of the United States of America, and are not Heirs in Law or by birthright, i.e. Posterity, and have caused grievous harm, damage and injury under pretense and color of law, and are in breach of numerous legal duties imposed upon our Public Offices, they (the Accused) by Law are barred, estopped and precluded, under the "Clean Hands doctrine," and "Public Policy", from making any claim of right, title, or interest thereon. (See: 18 USCS 1001).

42 • The letterhead of the IRS NOTICES OF LEVY and business cards state that they are documents of "Department of the Treasury - Internal Revenue Service"; however, the Department of Justice letterhead says: "U.S. Department of Justice - Tax Division".

43 • The Defendants are not officers or employees or assignees of the United States Government.

44 • The IRS is not an organization within the United States Department of the Treasury.

45 • There is no organic Act creating the IRS as a lawful organization.

46 • The IRS is a collection agency working for foreign banks and operating out of Puerto Rico under color of the Federal Alcohol Administration (FAA).

47 • The FAA was promptly declared unconstitutional inside the 50 States by the U.S. Supreme Court in the case of U.S. v. Constantine, 296 U.S. 287 (1935) when Prohibition was repealed.

48 • There is no legal authority for the IRS to establish offices inside the 50 States of the Union.

49 • The IRS can not legally show "Department of the Treasury" on their outgoing mail.

50 • The U.S. Department of Justice does not have power of attorney to represent the IRS in federal court.

51 • The IRS is domiciled in Puerto Rico.

52 • The so-called 14th and 16th amendments were not properly ratified.

53 • There are no statutes that create a specific liability for federal income taxes, except for government employees pursuant to the Public Salary Tax Act.

54 • A federal regulation can not create a specific liability when no specific liability is created by the corresponding statute.

55 • An administrative agency can not create a criminal offense or any liability not sanctioned by the lawmaking authority.

56 • Federal regulations create an income tax liability for only TWO classes of people: federal citizens and federal employees.

57 • One can be a state citizen without being a federal citizen.

58 • State citizens are nonresident aliens with respect to the municipal jurisdiction of Congress, i.e. the federal zone.

59 • A "withholding agent" is one who is authorized by an employee to withhold part of his wages.

60 • The payroll officer does not have "permission" or "power of attorney" to withhold taxes from workers who do not "authorize" or "allow" withholding by knowingly, intentionally, and voluntarily signing an IRS Form W4.

61 • A properly executed Form W4 creates the presumption that the worker wishes to be treated as

if he were an "employee" of the federal government.

62 • A "Withholding Exemption Certificate" can be personally created and executed as an alternative to Form W4 in lieu of a Form W4.

63 • Filing a Form W4 is not mandatory for workers who are not "employed" by the federal government.

64 • Protesting the claims of the IRS is Not "tax evasion".

65 • Only "taxpayers" can be found guilty of "tax evasion."

66 • Corporations chartered by the 50 States of the Union are technically "foreign" corporations with respect to the IRC.

67 • Congress has no authority to create a national corporation.

68 • The IRS does not require a Notary Public to notarize a taxpayer's signature on a Form 1040, even though Congress mandates that written verifications must be executed under penalty of perjury and a Notary Public as a witness to one's signature.

69 • The terms "United States" and "United States of America" do not refer to the same entity.

70 • Verifications executed "outside the "United States" (the federal zone) are executed "inside the States of the Union.

71 • The term "United States" has multiple legal meanings; geographical, political, territorial.

72 • The term "income" is not defined in the IRC.

73 • The term "income" means the profit or gain derived from corporate activity under the corporate privilege of limited liability.

74 • Income tax provisions do not constitute Municipal law.

75 • Municipal law is law that is enacted to govern the internal affairs of a sovereign State.

76 • Municipal law in legal circles is also known as

Private International Law.

77 • The Internal Revenue Code is Not a Municipal Revenue Code.

78 • The State of Maine is not mentioned in any of the federal income tax statutes.

79 • Congress has no authority to exercise a power that is not enumerated in the U.S. Constitution.

80 • No federal income tax statute has any force or effect within the State of Maine.

81 • Vagueness is sufficient grounds for concluding that the entire IRS Code is unconstitutional, null, and void.

82 • The entire IRS Code is unconstitutional, null, and void for violating our fundamental Right to know the nature and cause of any accusation as guaranteed by the Sixth Amendment in the Bill of Rights.

83 • Title 26 of the United States Code was never enacted into positive law.

84 • Federal courts are not authorized to prosecute income tax crimes.

85 • Constitutional District Courts of the United States ("DC.US") are not the same as legislative United States District Courts ("US.DC").

86 • Federal judges are not required to pay income taxes on their pay.

87 • Federal judges routinely rule in favor of the IRS because they fear the retaliation that might result from ruling against the IRS.

88 • Federal grand juries can not issue valid indictments against illegal tax protesters.

89 • IRS agents tamper with federal grand juries by misrepresenting themselves, under oath, as lawful employees and "special agents" of the federal government.

90 • IRS agents tamper with federal grand juries by acting as if "income" is everything that "comes in";

when there is no such definition anywhere in the IR Code.

91 • Bank signature cards constitute competent waivers of their customers' fundamental rights to privacy, as secured by the Fourth and Fifth Amendments.

92 • The income tax provisions have No legal force or effect inside the 50 States of the Union.

93 • Income tax provisions are forms of perjury, and possibly misprision of perjury by ommission, which are serious federal offenses.

94 • There is ample evidence to indicate that IRS agents bribe U.S. Attorneys, federal judges, and even the Office of the President with huge kickbacks every time a criminal indictment is issued by a federal grand jury against an illegal tax protester.

95 • The IRS is a federal government subcontractor and a private Puerto Rico Trust.

96 • The IRS cannot lawfully levy personal property, or bank accounts, without Notice, a Hearing, and due process of law resulting in a valid warrant or court order.

97 • No government services are funded by federal income taxes.

98 • The final report of the Grace Commission, convened under President Ronald Reagan, quietly admitted that none of the funds they collect from federal income taxes goes to pay for any government services.

99 • The availability of correct information about federal government operations is fundamental to maintaining the freedom of the American People.

100 • No statutes create a specific liability for taxes imposed by subtitle A of the IRC.

101 • Americans are being misled to believe that the "Internal Revenue Service" is a United States organization.

102 • The "Internal Revenue Service" is not a United States organization nor is it part of any other country, state, county, or city.

103 • The IRS a private corporation incorporated in Delaware as a for-profit debt collection agency operating under the purview of Title 15 of the "US Code" and the "US Constitution" instead of Title 26 of the "IR Code".

104 • Title 15 of the US Code relates to "Verified Assessment" in that debt collectors are required to provide proof signed under penalty of perjury to validate any debt that debt collectors claim a person owes to the IRS.

105 • Debt collectors can not validate any debt that they claim is owed to the IRS in a documented response signed as a notarized affiant under the penalty of perjury.

106 • The IRS is not a part of the U.S. Government that can mail a letterhead that says: "U.S. Department of the Treasury - Internal Revenue Service".

107 • Liability for the individual income tax applies only to employees and agents of the U.S. Government and to those who manufacture and sell alcohol, tobacco, and fire arms, or other controlled substances.

108 • Liability for the individual income tax applies only to 14th Amendment citizens of the corporate United States and its territories and possessions.

109 • Any document made under Internal Revenue laws and regulations must contain or be verified by a written declaration made under the penalty of perjury according to Section 6065 of the Internal Revenue Code.

110 • The United States was declared bankrupt by President Roosevelt in June of 1933.

111 • The Internal Revenue Department of the United States Treasury is a separate entity from the Internal Revenue Service that is a collection agency of the non-federal Federal Reserve Bank.

112 • All obligations owing to the Internal Revenue Service can be discharged by a sovereign citizen through the United States Treasury per HJR 192 of June 5, 1933 upon one's presonal private demand.

113 • The IRS is not registered to do business or perform commercial matters in any state.

114 • People give the IRS money without demanding proof of claim, or even if the IRS is "licenced" to make commercial "offers" of credit based on "arbitrary" estimates.

115 • The IRS never has and never will issue a valid assessment in lien or levy form; such is not possible without affidavits sworn under the penalty of perjury and under commercial liability.

116 • A valid assessment requires a foundational instrument — a contract signed with the debtor's wet-ink autograph showing him in default.

117 • A valid assessment requires a list of the goods and services provided by the IRS, or of damages done.

118 • The fictitious entity called WILLIAM MESSIER is a federal government created corporation — as defined in 15 USCA § 44 (U.S. Code Annotated).

119 • William Messier's UCC Financing Statement gives public notice that he (the lawful man) has a claim against the debtor, WILLIAM MESSIER (the unincorporated strawman corporate trust) and all of his assets.

120 • F. William Messier has thereby taken this strawman entity "out of the state"; out of the jurisdiction of a fictitious entity into his private domain; thus the entity became an unincorporated corporate trust "foreign" to the state.

121 • William Messier's UCC Financing Statement shows that he has an enforceable security interest in the strawman debtor's property.

122 • F. William Messier's UCC Financing Statement is filed with the Secretary of State, and the Cumberland County Registra of deeds, and as such is a public record.

123 • The United States - US - U.S. - USA - America is a federal corporation under Title 28 USC 3002(5) Chapter 176.

124 • The United States is a corporation under 534 Federal Supplement 724.

125 • The United States is a corporation, originally incorporated February 21, 1871 under the name of "District of Columbia" per 16 Stat. 419 Chapter 62.

126 • The United States is a bankrupt organization per House Joint Resolution 192 of June 5, 1933; Senate Report 93-549; and Executive Orders 6072, 6102 and 6246.

127 • The United States is a de facto government; originally the ten square mile tract ceded by Maryland and Virginia comprising Washington, D.C. plus its possessions, territories, arsenals and forts.

128 • The United States, as a corporation, has no more authority to implement its laws against "We the People" than does the Mac Donald Corporation, — except for the unilateral contracts we've unknowingly signed as surety for our strawman with the United States and the foreign Creditor Bankers.

129 • The contracts we've signed as surety for our strawman with the United States and the foreign Creditor Bankers are actually not contracts with us, but with our artificial entity or "person", which appears to be us but is spelled with ALL CAPITAL LETTERS.

130 • The contracts we've signed as surety for our strawman with the United States and the foreign Creditor Bankers were done under Vice-Admiralty Courts established in the Queen's possessions beyond the seas, with jurisdiction over Maritime causes, including those relating to prize.

131 • The United States of America is lawfully the possession of the English Crown per original commercial joint venture agreement between the colonies and the Crown and the Constitution which brought all the states (only) back under British ownership and rule.

132 • The sovereign American people, however, had sovereign standing in law, independent of any connection to the states or the Crown.

133 • The sovereignty of the American people necessitated that the people be brought back under British Rule, one at a time, and the Commercial process was the method of choice in order to accomplish this recapturing task.

134 • This recapturing task was accomplished first through the 14th Amendment and then through the registration of our birth certificate and private property.

135 • All federal courts in America are Vice-Admiralty courts in the Crown's private commerce in this United States; the Queen's possession beyond the sea.

NOTICE OF LEVY - Form 668-A

IRS Forms **668-A** are deemed to be intentionally fraudulent and deceptive for the following reasons:

1. The heading **Department of the Treasury — Internal Revenue Service** does not show that the Department of the Treasury is not theDepartment of the Treasury of the United States; it 's the **Department of the Treasury of Puerto Rico**.

2. On the back of the form under the Heading **Sec. 6331. LEVY AND DISTRAINT** subsection (b) and (c) are shown but subsection (a) is intentionally missing.

US Code, Title 26, Subtitle F, Subchapter D Part II, **Section 6331 (a)** second sentence states:

> "Levy may be made upon the accrued salary or wages of any <u>officer</u>, <u>employee</u>, or <u>elected official</u>, of the United States, the District of Columbia, or any agency or instrumentality of the United States or the District of Columbia, by serving a notice of levy on the <u>employer</u> (as defined in section 3401(d)) of such officer, employee, or elected official."

Messier denies that he is or has ever been an officer, employee, or elected official, of the United States, the District of Columbia, or any agency or instrumentality of the United States or the District of Columbia therefore **Levy for taxes may NOT be made upon any kind or type of his income.**

What's more, Messier's customers are Not his <u>employers</u>; Messier is <u>self</u>-employed.

3. Messier has determined that the designation **"1040"** for the type of tax shown on the IRS' Notices of Federal Tax Liens that the IRS claims he is liable for does Not pertain to **Form 1040**; but misleadingly refers to **Section 1040** of the tax code under Subtitle B which pertains to **profit and gain on the Transfer by the <u>executor of an estate</u> of certain real property imposed upon the executor under <u>Section 1040 of the tax code.</u>**

The **1040 type of tax** is an **estate tax** that has nothing to do with Subtitle A of the tax code pertaining to income taxes.

In regard to the false verbal accusation of Jason S. Rogers (hereafter, "Rogers") regarding **26 USC 7212 - Attempt to interfere with administration of internal revenue laws**:

> **Re: Sect. 7212(a) Corrupt or forcible interference,** an honest request for discovery cannot be taken as Corrupt or forcible interference.

> **Re: Sect. 7212(b) Forcible rescue of seized property,** no property has been forcibly rescued or seized.

Congress never enacted **Title 26** as positive Law and **Title 26** is irrelevant to actions taken under **Title 15, the Fair Debt Collections Practices Act,** which pertains to Messier's defense herein and the IRS.

Messier's authority for making his demand for **verification of the Defendant's authority** has been well established as follows:

> "Whatever the form in which the Government functions, anyone entering into an arrangement with the Government takes the risk of having accurately ascertained that he who purports to act for the Government stays within the bounds of his authority... and this is so even though, as here, the agent himself may have been unaware of the limitations upon his authority." — *Federal Crop Insurance Corporation v. Merrill, 332 U.S. 380 at 384 (1947).*

Messier stands on the basis of **Title 15 USC 1692-1692p**—the **US Fair Debt Collection Practices Act**—and reserves his human rights.

WHAT THE DEFENDANTS FAILED TO PROVIDE

The Defendants failed to document their positions and authority by Not providing the following documents:

(1) the statutes that impose upon F. William Messier an obligation to provide any private personal papers to them.

(2) specific copies of their delegation orders from the Secretary down to the Commissioner, down to the District Director, and down to them.

(3) copies of any notices sent to F. William Messier that informed him that he is required to keep records and papers for the Secretary or the IRS or them; and produce such.

(4) copies of any determinations or decisions that show that F. William Messier is liable to the United States of America corporation or the IRS for any taxes.

(5) copies of any documents or decisions that show how F. William Messier came within the taxing authority of the corporate United States of America.

(6) Validation of any debt that the Defendants claim F. William Messier owes to the IRS, in a documented response signed as a notarized affiant under the penalty of perjury as is required by law.

(7) proof that the Accused are part of the U.S. Government and a letterhead that says U.S. Department of the Treasury - Internal Revenue Service if they are part of the U.S. Government.

(8) all documents on which the Defendants base their claim that F. William Messier has any obligation to the Accused or their Service or the corporate United States and that F. William Messier is required to produce books and records for their examination.

(9) copies of all documents that identify how F. William Messier comes within the purview of the statutes which they claim obligate him to produce personal documents for their examination.

(10) copies of all documents of determination that indicate F. William Messier is liable or subject to any statute that they or their Service claim to have authority to enforce.

(11) copies of all documents that identify the facts on which those determinations were made.

(12) copies of all statutes on which those facts were applied to make any of the determinations that F. William Messier is liable or subject.

(13) copies of the Notices sent or served upon F. William Messier prior to making those determinations.

(14) copies of their delegation of authority to inquire into F. William Messier's personal affairs or make any demand upon him or his customers, and the delegations of authority of those who made the above determinations that F. William Messier is liable or subject to those determinations.

(15) copies of the Defendants' document of appointment to the position which they now hold and copies of the documents that identify by name title, position, G.S.#, and office, each party who participated in any aspect of the above determinations.

(16) the document that describes the procedural format for expungement of alleged determinations, improperly or unlawfully made within and by their Service.

Without this specific documentation of authority F. William Messier presumes that none exists.

F. William Messier is in receipt of many form letter type NOTICES OF LEVY from the agency that the Accused serve, that carry a stamped signature (or no signature at all) which claims that an IRS agent has been assigned to examine alleged federal tax returns of his.

The Accused are in error and proceeding on false assumptions if they believe that F. William Messier has some obligation of tax liability to them or the Internal Revenue Service, debt collection agency of the non-federal Federal Reserve Bank.

F. William Messier gave each of the Defendants NOTICE of those errors and he declared his objection to any such presumed claims by them or anyone else in their Internal Revenue Service. F. William Messier denies that he has any obligation of tax liability to the Accused or to the IRS.

It is F. William Messier's intention to obey all laws that legitimately impose a requirement or obligation upon him. However, he has no desire to volunteer where no obligation exists, especially when the waiver of his rights is involved. He is relying on what the Supreme Court held long ago:

> "An individual may be under no obligation to do a particular thing, and his failure to act creates no liability; but if he voluntarily attempts to act and do a particular thing, he comes under an implied obligation in respect to the manner in which he does it." Guardian T&D Co. v. Fisher (1906) 26 S.Ct. 186,188.

Therefore, F. William Messier has determined that he is not one of the Accused's subjects. Neither is he one to whom they can demand that he produce personal documents and records for their review or that he has any obligation to submit those records for an examination by them or others for any purpose.

What's more, F. William Messier has determined that the designation "1040" for the type of tax shown on the IRS' Notices of Federal Tax Liens that the IRS claims he is liable for does not pertain to Form 1040; but misleadingly refers to Section 1040 of the tax code under Subtitle B which pertains to profit and gain on the Transfer by the executor of an estate of certain real property imposed upon the executor under Section 1040 of the tax code which is an estate tax that has nothing to do with Subtitle A of the tax code referring to income taxes.

In regard to the Accused's false accusations regarding 26 USC Sect. 7212 - Attempt to interfere with administration of internal revenue laws:

Re: Sect. 7212(a) Corrupt or forcible interference, an honest request for discovery cannot be taken as Corrupt or forcible interference.

Re: Sect. 7212(b) Forcible rescue of seized property, no property has been forcibly rescued or seized.

Furthermore, Congress never enacted Title 26 as positive Law and Title 26 is irrelevant to action taken under Title 15 of the Fair Debt Collections Practices Act which pertains to F. William Messier's defense and the IRS.

26 USC § 7212 - Attempts to interfere with administration of IRS laws.

(a) Corrupt or forcible interference

Whoever corruptly or by force or threats of force (including any threatening letter or communication) endeavors to intimidate or impede any officer or employee of the United States acting in an official capacity under this title, or in any other way corruptly or by force or threats of force (including any threatening letter or communication) obstructs or impedes, or endeavors to obstruct or impede, the due administration of this title, shall, upon conviction thereof, be fined not more than $5,000, or imprisoned not more than 3 years, or both, except that if the offense is committed only by threats of force, the person convicted thereof shall be fined not more than $3,000, or imprisoned not more than 1 year, or both. The term "threats of force", as used in this subsection, means threats of bodily harm to the officer or employee of the United States or to a member of his family.

(b) Forcible rescue of seized property

Any person who forcibly rescues or causes

to be rescued any property after it shall have been seized under this title, or shall attempt or endeavor so to do, shall, excepting in cases otherwise provided for, for every such offense, be fined not more than $500, or not more than double the value of the property so rescued, whichever is the greater, or be imprisoned not more than 2 years.

F. William Messier's authority for making his demand for verification of the Accused's authority has been well established as follows:

"Whatever the form in which the Government functions, anyone entering into an arrangement with the Government takes the risk of having accurately ascertained that he who purports to act for the Government stays within the bounds of his authority... and this is so even though, as here, the agent himself may have been unaware of the limitations upon his authority." — Federal Crop Insurance Corporation v. Merrill, 332 U.S. 380 at 384 (1947).

F. William Messier stands on the basis of Title 15 U.S.C. Sections 1692-1692p — and reserved his human rights.

Section 805(b) COMMUNICATION WITH THIRD PARTIES: "without the prior consent of the consumer a debt collector may not communicate with any person other than a consumer, etc."

Section 807(1) False or misleading representations: "A debt collector may not use any false, deceptive or mis-leading representation or means in connection with the collection of any debt."

(1) "The false implication that the debt collector is affiliated with the United States..."

(2) "The false representation of (A) the character of any debt..."

Messier offered to settle this matter out of court by the Accused ceasing collection activities and returning his funds **without further penalty to them** personally and the Accused failed to respond to his offer by correcting their faults by the prompt return of his funds in lieu of the documents requested above.

Messier did Not hear from the Accused within the time period offered so their *lack of response established the presumption that they do not have the documentation or the authority to support their claim* — establishing BREACH OF CONTRACT.

TIMELY NOTICE AND DEMAND HAS BEEN GIVEN THEM (18 U.S.C.S. 4, 2382)

Testified by F. William Messier AND David E. Robinson on the 3rd day of August, in the year of our Lord 2012 under the penalty of perjury.

To Whom It May Concern:

I am writing, for the fourth time, to report the criminal conduct of the "INTERNAL REVENUE SERVICE", for the "Racketeering Activity" of "interference with commerce" 18 USC 1951, "Extortionate Credit Transactions" 18 USC 891-894 and "Conspiracy against rights" 18 USC 241 . The "INTERNAL REVENUE SERVICE" has been informed of the law and they have refused to comply by unlawfully imposing a levy on the income of the Principal **David Anderson** without due process of law. The United States Code clearly establishes "Due Process for Collections" 26 USC 6330. No notice was given for this levy (Attached) and it is a levy on income to collect a debt that by Federal Law is paid in full. The common practice of this "Organized Crime" is clear, **one office of the IRS accepts payment in full, then another office of the IRS levies against the property of that person and collects the debt yet again without any due process of law.**

LAWFUL STATUS:

The "INTERNAL REVENUE SERVICE" is incorporated in Delaware as a collection agency for a Puerto Rico Company; "INTERNAL REVENUE TAX AND AUDIT" (IRS)/// For Profit General Corporation /// Incorporated date 7/12/33 /// File No. 0325720.

Therefore, the "INTERNAL REVENUE SERVICE" must be recognized in its lawful status as a "Collection Agency" and not fraudulently accepted as a "government agency". This "Corporation" is accountable under Title 15 of the United States Codes Section 1692e. A debt collector may not use false, deceptive or misleading representation. **It is the common misconception, that the "INTERNAL REVENUE SERVICE" is part of the United States Government, but in fact it is a "Private Corporation".** This "Corporation" is now brought before all members of "Congress" to establish their authority under our laws.

Through fraud, manipulation, conspiracy, deceit and impersonation of law enforcement personnel, the IRS has become an "Organized Crime Syndicate" operating in every State of this union. There are three major elements of this "Organized Crime" these are as follows:

1. "Extortionate Credit Transactions" 18 USC 891-894

This is the common practice of "IRS Agents" to threaten, coerce, intimidate and force the people to pay a "Debt" that the IRS generates out of thin air and can not lawfully establish. There is no due process of law allowed. Those who oppose the tax are prosecuted by US Attorneys who are more than willing to engage in "Conspiracy Against Rights" 18 USC 241 for the profits they receive from the money they "Extort" within the Fraud 18 USC 1001 of claiming to collect a debt that is owed. In fact no debt to the IRS can be lawfully established. It can not be lawfully established that an "American Citizen" owes this corporation anything, all claims that they do are "Fraud".

2. "Seizure of Property without Due Process" Violation 4th Amendment

It has become the common practice of the IRS to file "Levies" against Personal property without any judicial process. These levies are filed with the "Recorder of Deeds" who has established the common practice of allowing "levies" of the IRS to be recorded without a "Judgment" signed by a judge which is lawfully required for

DAVID E. ROBINSON, INTERIM ATTORNEY GENERAL FOR THE MAINE FREE STATE
3 LINNELL CIRCLE, BRUNSWICK, MAINE 04011

May 16, 2012

This "Request for Discovery" is in regard to the fraudulent IRS **NOTICES OF LIEN** being sent to you by the IRS against **F. WILLIAM MESSIER**, 40 Tower Lane, Brunswick ME 04011.

DEAR ACCOUNTS PAYABLE,

The **Federal Reserve** is no more a federal agency than is **Federal Express!**
The **Internal Revenue Service** in no more a federal agency than is **Dagget & Parker, or McDonalds!**

The "**Internal Revenue Service**" is incorporated in Delaware as a "collection agency" for a Puerto Rican Company titled "Internal Revenue Tax & Audit Service" (IRS) — a for-profit corporation — Incorporated on 07/12/33 — File No. 0325720.

Therefore the "**Internal Revenue Service**" must be recognized in its lawful status as a "**DEBT COLLECTION AGENCY**" and not be fraudulently accepted as a "**Government Agency**".

A "**Notice of Levy**" is not a "**Levy**"! — In dealing with an **IRS "debt collector" Agent (or any other "debt collector")** the following **Seven items** of information need to be obtained for "**Proof of Claim**".

(1) **Ask** the IRS Agent for a copy of his "**DRIVER'S LICENSE**" to verify that he is who he says he is. You need to record the "**License Number**" for possible use in case he has to be served with legal papers, so he can be located for proper service.

(2) **Ask** the IRS Agent for a copy of his "**POCKET COMMISSION MANUAL**" showing his "authority to act" in this case. The most common type is "**Administrator**" (**type A**). The second type is "**Enforcer**" (**type E**). Administrators can only shuffle the paperwork. They cannot enforce the IRS law.

(3) **Ask** the IRS Agent for a copy of the "**ACTUAL ASSESSMENT**" — **NOT the 668-A Notice of Levy** — showing what the IRS claims the alleged "taxpayer" owes — according to the **Internal Revenue**, that the **Internal Revenue Service** is authorized to collect.

(4) **Ask** the IRS Agent for a copy of the "**ABSTRACT OF COURT JUDGMENT**" that verifies that the alleged "taxpayer" has a **Jury Trial** before any of his assets could be seized.

(5) **Demand** that the IRS Agent **confirm all of his written answers under the penalty of perjury.**

(6) **Demand** that the IRS Agent **provide you with a copy of the "missing part (a)" (of Section 6331 "Levy and Distraint") missing on the back of the 668-A "Notice of Levy".**

(7) **Ask** the IRS Agent which "**Title**" he is operating under — **Title 26 of the "IR Code"** or **Title 15 of the "US Code" regarding corporations.**

The **Internal Revenue (IR)** is a government agency under **Title 26 of the "IR Code" Manual.**

The **Internal Revenue Service (IRS)** is a **private foreign for-profit "debt-collection agency"** — **it is not connected with any government** — it operates under **Title 15 of the "US Code".**

By sending **Mr. F. William Messier's Property (his money)** to the IRS **without judicial process of law and without first having verified the AUTHENTICITY of the IRS Agent's claims,** you may be liable to **PROSECUTION** for having committed illegal **"CONVERSION OF PROPERTY" — which is a second degree felony punishable by a fine and/or imprisonment or both.**

Debt-collection agencies are subject to **Title 15 of the United States Code** relating to **"Verified Assessment"** whereby the **"Debt Collection Agency" (of which you are now a debt-collector extension)** must provide **"proof of the claim"** to validate the debt.

Any case involving the collection of debt must have been adjudicated in a local judicial district court.

The IRS has no way to verify an alleged debt without the alleged "taxpayer" voluntarily assessing himself.

According to **Title 15, Section 1692,** a debt-collector...
1. **must legally identify himself;**
2. **must not state that the consumer owes any debt;**
3. **must not use any symbol that indicates that he is in the debt-collection business;**
4. **must not imply that he is affiliated with the United States Government or any of the states.**

It is obvious that the IRS Agent has NOT obeyed these legal requirements in this case.

Please acknowledge the receipt of this letter by sending an email from a company contact to:
    F. William Messier <k1mnw@yahoo.com>
    David E. Robinson <drobin88@comcast.net>

Obtain Copies of the **(7) Items of Verification** listed above from IRS "DEBT-COLLECTION AGENT" **JOLINE P. HENDERSHOT**, 217 MAIN STREET, LEWISTON ME 04240, and from IRS "DEBT-COLLECTION AGENT" **PATRICK FRIE**, 220 MAINE MALL ROAD, SOUTH PORTLAND ME 04106 **and send duplicate copies, and copies of all correspondence sent to you from the IRS, to me by snail mail, to the above letterhead-address, within the next twenty (20) days from your receipt of this Demand.** More time will be granted upon your written request. **Failure to timely comply will be taken as material evidence that you refuse to honor this Demand.**

I await your timely response.

                    Sincerely,

                    David E. Robinson
                    Interim Attorney General for the Maine Free State

Attached:

Maine Republic Email Newsletter Alerts:
    087 The Internal Revenue is not the Internal Revenue Service
    088 Nil-dicit Judgment ("he says nothing" judgment)
    090 IRS Levis and Liens
    094 IRS Strategy
    095 Internal Revenue Service Personnel

26 USC § 6331 - Levy and distraint
THE MISSING Par. (a) from NOTICE OF LEVY

Par. (a) Authority of Secretary

If any person **liable to pay any tax** neglects or refuses to pay the same within 10 days after notice and demand, it shall be lawful for the **Secretary** to collect such tax (and such further sum as shall be sufficient to cover the expenses of the levy) by levy upon all property and rights to property (except such property as is exempt under section 6334) belonging to such person or on which there is a lien provided in this chapter for the payment of such tax.

Levy may be made upon the accrued salary or wages of any officer, employee, or elected official, of the United States, the District of Columbia, or any agency or instrumentality of the United States or the District of Columbia, by serving a notice of levy on the employer (as defined in section 3401(d)) **of such officer, employee, or elected official.**

If the **Secretary** makes a finding that the collection of such tax is in jeopardy, notice and demand for immediate payment of such tax may be made by the Secretary and, upon failure or refusal to pay such tax, collection thereof by levy shall be lawful without regard to the 10-day period provided in this section.

NOTE
(27 CFR 250.11 Definitions)
"**Secretary** means Secretary of the Treasury of Puerto Rico."

Note

Paraphrased:

"**Levy may only be made upon the accrued salary or wages of officers, employees, or elected officials, of the United States, the District of Columbia, or any agency or instrumentality of the United States or the District of Columbia.**"

VIOLATIONS OF THE U.S. FAIR DEBT COLLECTION PRACTICES ACT

The following Sections of THE U.S. FAIR DEBT COLLECTION PRACTICES ACT (15 USC §§ 1692-1692p) have been violated.

§ 804 - Acquisition of location information:
Any debt collector communicating with any person other than the consumer for the purpose of acquiring location information about the consumer:

§ 804(2) ...shall not state that such Consumer owes any debt.

§ 804(5) ...shall not use any language or symbol...that indicates that the debt collector...is in the debt collection business or that the communication relates to the collection of a debt.

§ 805 Communication in connection with debt collection
§ 805(b) Communication With Third Parties. Without the prior consent of the consumer given directly to the debt collector, or the express permission of a court of competent jurisciction, ... a debt collector may not communicate ... with any person other than a consumer, his attorney ... etc.

§ 807 False or misleading representations
A debt collector may not use any false, deceptive, or misleading representation or means in connection with the collection of any debt... the following conduct is a violation of this section:

§ 807(1) The false representation or implication that the debt collector is vouched for, bonded by, or affiliated with the United States ...

§ 807(2) The false representation of (A) the character of legal stautus of any debt.

§ 807(13) The false representation or implication that his documents are legal process.

CIVIL DAMAGES FOR UNAUTHORIZED COLLECTION ACTIONS - 26 USC 7433 -

(a) In general

If, in connection with any collection of Federal tax with respect to a taxpayer, any officer or employee of the Internal Revenue Service recklessly or intentionally, or by reason of negligence, disregards any provision of this title, or any regulation promulgated under this title, such taxpayer may bring a civil action for damages against the United States in a district court of the United States.

Except as provided in section 7432, such civil action shall be the exclusive remedy for recovering damages resulting from such actions.

(b) Damages

In any action brought under subsection (a) or petition filed under subsection (e), upon a finding of liability on the part of the defendant, the defendant shall be liable to the plaintiff in an amount equal to the lesser of $1,000,000 ($100,000, in the case of negligence) or the sum of—

(1) actual, direct economic damages sustained by the plaintiff as a proximate result of the reckless or intentional or negligent actions of the officer or employee, and

(2) the costs of the action.

(c) Payment authority

Claims pursuant to this section shall be payable out of funds appropriated under section 1304 of title 31, United States Code.

(d) Limitations

(1) Requirement that administrative remedies be exhausted

A judgment for damages shall not be awarded under subsection (b) unless the court determines that the plaintiff has exhausted the administrative remedies available to such plaintiff within the Internal Revenue Service.

(2) Mitigation of damages

The amount of damages awarded under subsection (b)(1) shall be reduced by the amount of such damages which could have reasonably been mitigated by the plaintiff.

(3) Period for bringing action

Notwithstanding any other provision of law, an action to enforce liability created under this section may be brought without regard to the amount in controversy and may be brought only within 2 years after the date the right of action accrues.

(e) Actions for violations of certain bankruptcy procedures

(1) In general

If, in connection with any collection of Federal tax with respect to a taxpayer, any officer or employee of the Internal Revenue Service willfully violates any provision of section 362 (relating to automatic stay) or 524 (relating to effect of discharge) of title 11, United States Code (or any successor provision), or any regulation promulgated under such provision, such taxpayer may petition the bankruptcy court to recover damages against the United States.

(2) Remedy to be exclusive

(A) In general

Except as provided in subparagraph (B), notwithstanding section 105 of such title 11, such petition shall be the exclusive remedy for recovering damages resulting from such actions.

(B) Certain other actions permitted

Subparagraph (A) shall not apply to an action under section 362(h) of such title 11 for a violation of a stay provided by section 362 of such title; except that—

(i) administrative and litigation costs in connection with such an action may only be awarded under section 7430; and

(ii) administrative costs may be awarded only if incurred on or after the date that the bankruptcy petition is filed.

VALIDATION OF DUE PROCESS

The weak link in our property rights is at the heart of how the IRS continues to successfully collect a tax that few Americans actually owe.

This unethical application of the tax laws is called **violation of due process**, and it is quite commonplace.

The federal courts, however, have said that the issue of a "Notice of Levy" does not constitute a valid levy.

This is one example:

A "levy" requires that property be brought into legal custody through seizure, actual or constructive, levy being an absolute appropriation in law of property levied on, and mere notice of intent to levy is insufficient.

— *United States v. O'Dell, 6 Cir., 1947, 160 F.2d 304, 307. Accord, In re Holdsworth, D.C.N.J. 1953, 113 F.Supp. 878, 888; United States v. Aetna Life Ins. Co. of Hartford, Conn., D.C.Conn. 1942, 146 F.Supp. 30, 37,*

— in **which Judge Hincks observed that he could "find no statute which says that a mere notice shall constitute a 'levy.'"**

There are cases which hold that a <u>warrant for distraint</u> is necessary to constitute a levy.

— *Givan v. Cripe, 7 Cir., 1951, 187 F.2d 225; United States v. O'Dell, supra.*

The Court of Appeals for the Third Circuit state in is opinion, 221 F.2d at page 642, **"These sections [26 U.S.C. §§3690-3697] require that levy by a deputy collector be accompanied by warrants of distraint** [issued by a judge in a legal proceeding]." — *In re: Brokol Manufacturing Co., supra.*

The IRS often deceives financial institutions and county recorders throughout the nation into surrendering property of taxpayers by issuing fraudulent "Notice of Levy" or lien documents.

These fraudulent Notices of Levy, printed on **IRS Form 668-A** quote portions of 26 U.S.C. 6331 *but conveniently leave out paragraph (a), which specifically says that the levy can only occur against employees of the federal government.*

The clerks of employers and financial institutions who receive these levies usually have no legal training and will just surrender the money or property of the accused without asking even a single question.

They won't even verify that the levy or lien is signed by a magistrate.

Oftentimes, they are threatened by the IRS with an audit or levy or seizure of their own if they did comply

War is an extremely lucrative business for the bankers of the New World Order. Loans for destruction. Loans for re-construction. Loans for controlling people on her world property.

The purpose of the IRS is not to collect taxes but to terrorize and control.

Everyone knows that the politicians have been bought and have sold out the People to the banksters.

The Business of Government is Fraud, Racketeering, Embezzlement, Extortion and Treason.

Subject: 26 U.S.C. 6331 but conveniently leave out paragraph (a): Levy can only occur against employees of the federal government.

No Lien or Notice of Levy issued by the IRS is valid unless accompanied by a court order signed by a magistrate.

If these forms have nothing but the unsigned name of an IRS employee on them, they are a fraud!

26 USC § 7214
OFFENSES BY OFFICERS AND EMPLOYEES
OF THE UNITED STATES

7214(a) Unlawful acts of revenue officers or agents

Any officer or employee of the United States acting in connection with any revenue law of the United States—

(1) who is guilty of any extortion or willful oppression under color of law; or

(2) who knowingly demands other or greater sums than are authorized by law, or receives any fee, compensation, or reward, except as by law prescribed, for the performance of any duty; or

(3) who with intent to defeat the application of any provision of this title fails to perform any of the duties of his office or employment; or

(4) who conspires or colludes with any other person to defraud the United States; or

(5) who knowingly makes opportunity for any person to defraud the United States; or

(6) who does or omits to do any act with intent to enable any other person to defraud the United States; or

(7) who makes or signs any fraudulent entry in any book, or makes or signs any fraudulent certificate, return, or statement; or

(8) who, having knowledge or information of the violation of any revenue law by any person, or of fraud committed by any person against the United States under any revenue law, fails to report, in writing, such knowledge or information to the Secretary; or

(9) who demands, or accepts, or attempts to collect, directly or indirectly as payment or gift, or otherwise, any sum of money or other thing of value for the compromise, adjustment, or settlement of any charge or complaint for any violation or alleged violation of law, except as expressly authorized by law so to do;

. . . shall be dismissed from office or discharged from employment and, upon conviction thereof, shall be fined not more than $10,000, or imprisoned not more than 5 years, or both. The court may in its discretion award out of the fine so imposed an amount, not in excess of one-half thereof, for the use of the informer, if any, who shall be ascertained by the judgment of the court. The court also shall render judgment against the said officer or employee for the amount of damages sustained in favor of the party injured, to be collected by execution.

(b) Interest of internal revenue officer or employee in tobacco or liquor production

Any internal revenue officer or employee interested, directly or indirectly, in the manufacture of tobacco, snuff, or cigarettes, or in the production, rectification, or redistillation of distilled spirits, shall be dismissed from office; and each such officer or employee so interested in any such manufacture or production, rectification, or redistillation or production of fermented liquors shall be fined not more than $5,000.

(c) Cross reference

For penalty on collecting or disbursing officers trading in public funds or debts of property, see 18 U.S.C. 1901.

UNREFUTTED FACTS RE: THE UNITED STATES

1. The IRS (a Private Corporation) has NO authority to Take by Force any records, property, money, or thing of value, without a Court Order from a United States District Court.

2. Citizens do not have to respond to a request for documents, an Order to Produce Documents, or a Summons from the IRS, which is not issued under Court Order.

3. This ruling also applies to all third party agencies and persons, and includes all administrative orders and directives.

4. **31 USC** is the designated US Code section for Tax Regulations and Administration of the U.S. Treasury Department Operations.

5. Subsequent regulatory administration activities are covered by Treasury Orders from the Treasury Secretary.

6. Several sections within 31 U.S.C. state explicitly that Authority may only be delegated to subordinates by the Treasury Secretary through Executive Treasury Orders.

7. **Public Law 94-455** in 1976 further clarified this, specifically requiring all Regulations and Internal Revenue Code Sections be amended to reflect that only the Treasury Secretary had the Authority to take enforcement actions, and carry out Administration of all Treasury functions, and that any Delegation of Authority had to be by Treasury Order.

8. A close review of **31 U.S.C.** discloses that the Internal Revenue Service, a Private Corporation, **is not shown as a division, bureau, or any part of the U.S. Treasury Department.**

9. **31 U.S.C. Chapter 3** does not list the IRS as an agency or part of the Treasury Department.

10. **31 U.S.C. Subtitle VI section 9101** does not show the IRS as a Government Owned Corporation under "Government Corporations ".

11. **31 U.S.C. Subtitle I Chapter 9 section 901** does not list the IRS as an authorized agency.

12. The Internal Revenue Service lists it's Authority for operation as **Internal Revenue Code section 7801** in many of the IRS publications.

13. **IRC 7801** does not say one word about the **IRS,** only the **ATF** and the **US Justice Department.**

14. The IRC is not statutory law in any case, and cannot serve to authorize any Agency.

15. **Sections 7801, 7802, 7803** of the IRC are Administrative Sections, added by the IRS Special Council, and are not supported by any CFR, and are not "Law".

16. Only **CFR** or **U.S.C.** is Law which are promulgated by Acts of the US Congress through Public Law passage.

17. There are **two different things** called the "Internal Revenue Code".

18. The official **Internal Revenue Code** is imbedded in the **5 books of Federal Tax Regulations**, with the correct Citation and Enactment into Law cited in Section 1.1-1 as required.

19. This is the **Internal Revenue Code** derived by Public Law 951 in 1954.

20. There is a **sixth Book** entitled **Internal Revenue Code, Volume 68A,** published by the IRS, which is **a reference book** of IRS Interpretations of what the CFR and USC underlying Law requires; it is a **Novel**, and most sections are not conforming to the requirements of the CFR requirements, or the Federal Tax Regulations 5 books.

21. None of these Books are positive Statute Law, because Public Law 951 never made them so.

22. Only CFR or USC sections are Law, and an Internal Revenue Code Section can only be considered valid as implementing regulations where it is directly supported by CFR or USC sections, word for word.

Complaint and Motion for Summary Judgement or Jury Trial

23. The **5 books of the Federal Tax Regulations** cannot be considered valid at this point as they deliberately have not been updated with the requirements and Law sections passed by congress since 1976.

24. Sections which make it more convenient for the Treasury or specifically the IRS to continue fleecing American citizens have been updated, but not sections affected by Public Laws intended to correct the misapplication of the laws by the IRS.

25. The IRS was not established by any Act of the US Congress, as most of the US Government Agencies and boards and Commissions have been.

26. The Act of Congress in each case spells out specifically the rights and responsibilities, organizational structure, methods of regulations issue and approval, where the organization fits within the US Federal Government structure, and whether it is to operate autonomously or as part of another divisional structure.

27. **The Internal Revenue Service is a private Collections Company, acting as a permanent contractor for the US Treasury department, without any Legal Statute authorization.**

28. The IRS says that the Internal Revenue Code (the Novel, Book 68A) gives them the Authority to operate, and that it regulates its activities.

29. **Treasury Order 150-10** delegates Authority to the **Commissioner of Internal Revenue** (a US Government Employee) to administrate implementation of the Internal Revenue Code, **but makes no mention of the Internal Revenue Service, a private company.**

30. In **IRC** (Book 68A) **section 7802**, an appointed Oversight Board is authorized, which can make recommendations on appointments, and makes reports to congress, **but has no actual Oversight Authority over the operations of the IRS.**

31. The appointed Commissioner of Internal Revenue, and Deputy Commissioners, the Special Coun-

cil to the IRS (and staff), and the Taxpayer Advocate are US Government employees.

32. **All other IRS personnel work for the Internal Revenue Service, a Private Company contractor.**

33. There is NO CFR supporting **IRC 7802**, it is an administrative Section, added to the IRC by the Special Council.

34. The IRS, in internal publications says it can be an authorized contractor by IRC (Book 68A) section 7803, which references 5 USC section 3109 (b).

35. There is no supporting CFR for IRC section 7803, therefore **it is Administrative, and is not Law.**

36. **5 USC 3109(b)** only provides for Temporary and Intermittent Services to be contracted by Federal Agencies.

37. There is no Public Law which ever established that government Services could be permanently "Privatized", which is the very reason that Congress has been trying desperately for 6 sessions to pass a law to allow Privatization of Government functions.

38. No Public Law ever allowed the Privatization of Tax Administration and collections.

39. Since the IRS was not established by Act of Congress, or approved for implementation by Statute Law, it has no authority whatever to interpret the CFR and USC Laws, **which it does with no authority.**

40. No US Treasury Order delegates any authority to the Internal Revenue Service.

41. Neither the **Internal Revenue Code** (in the **5 books of the Federal Tax Regulations**, the official one) not the Novel reference **IRC Book 68A** are statute Law, but promulgated rules of implementation, and cannot by themselves confer any authority not specifically found in CFR or USC supporting Law.

42. It is illegal to refer to the **Internal Revenue Code** in a public court document, indictment, or

publication, as **26 USC** (it is violation of **18 USC 241** and **18 USC 1018**) as it has never been made such by Public Law in an Act of Congress.

43. The contracting of the IRS by the US Department of the Treasury is problematic, in that the stated **5 USC Section 3109(b)** allows only for **"Temporary and Intermittent Services"** of contractors to supplement US Government personnel.

44. There is no supporting CFR section **to authorize IRC 7802,** so it is administrative in nature.

45. **There is no Statute which allows the privatization of Government Tax Administration.**

46. There are multiple sections of USC which regulate and control the use of contractors, contract proposals, bidding, and transparency of the process.

47. All these provisions have apparently been bypassed, and **USC completely disregarded.**

48. FOIA Requests to the Treasury Department for the contract between the Treasury Department and the Internal Revenue Service will not be responded to except with rubbish that it is classified, and it is not subject to the FOIA requirements.

49. FOIA Requests to the Internal Revenue Service **for a copy of their Corporate Charter,** will similarly be responded that **it is privileged internal administrative data,** and not subject to the FOIA.

50. FOIA Requests to the IRS on what authorizes their activities in Statute Law, come back with the same frivolous gibberish, that their activities are authorized by the Internal Revenue Code.

51. FOIA for the Delegation Orders from the Secretary of the Treasury to the IRS for authorization to Implement and Collect the tax programs get the same no answers.

52. FOIA Requests to the IRS for the Delegation Order from the Commissioner of Internal Revenue to the Commissioner of the Internal Revenue Service to implement the administration and collection of US Government Taxes, are only responded to with frivolous gibberish that they are unnecessary, as it is all contained in the Internal Revenue Code.

53. The IRS will not define which of the Internal Revenue Code versions is the official version, Book 68A which is the reference book, or the official version in the **5 books of Federal Tax Regulations**.

54. **Only the Internal Revenue Code version in the 5 Books of Federal Tax Regulations has the required legal citations.**

55. **Federal Jurisdiction: — The zone** of Federal Jurisdiction, where the U.S. Federal Government has exclusive legislative authority, **is within the District of Columbia, Guam, American Samoa, Puerto Rico and the other American Offshore Territories and possessions, and under admiralty Law in the territorial waters off the continental coasts,** (federal zone) outside of the territorial waters controlled by the states (state zone waters).

56. **No Federal Legislative Jurisdiction lies within the borders of the 50 States.**

57. Federal rules, laws, and jurisdiction can only be applied within the 50 states borders **with written permission from the state, for designated Federal Forts, Magazines, Interstate Waterways, and Buildings.**

58. **This clearly prohibits the Internal Revenue Code from any application <u>outside</u> of the zone of Exclusive Federal Jurisdiction, and <u>prohibits</u> its application <u>within</u> the borders of the 50 states.**

59. Without constitutional amendment, **this also clearly prohibits any Federal Contractor (IRS) from exerting any jurisdiction within the borders of the 50 states.**

60. United States Constitution, **Article 1, Section 8, clause 17;** implementing statute **40 USC part 7, section 7(3).**

61. **7(a). Citations:** Supreme Court : *Spreckles Sugar Refining Co. v. McClain,* 192 US 397, page 416; A Citizen is exempt from Taxation, unless the same is imposed by Statute in clear and unequivocal language.

62. So clearly, per this Supreme Court ruling, and the United States Constitution, **no Implementing Regulation, such as the Internal Revenue Code, in either form** (imbedded in the Federal Tax Regulations 5 books) **or the IRS Novel** (Book 68A) **can Impose any Tax.**

63. **A Tax may be imposed only by Statute Law (CFR or USC) which is specifically codified from Public Laws passed by the United States Congress.**

64. Supreme Court: *Gould v. Gould,* 245 U.S. 150 (1917) ruled that: **The Government, in any agency, cannot apply or implicate that one portion of US Code can apply to another US Code section subject matter or application.**

65. So clearly, **IRC sections** supported by **27 CFR** for alcohol, tobacco, and firearms cannot be used for **26 CFR activities and subject matter.**

66. **There are no penalty provisions in 26 CFR regarding Income Taxes.**

67. **There are no sections of 18 USC addressing non-payment of Income Taxes, or non-filing of returns.**

68. There are no sections of 28 USC allowing the IRS to investigate or make submittal of criminal information and complaints to the USDJ, as the Federal District Courts have no Criminal subject matter Jurisdiction for 26 CFR.

69. Congress only gave the Federal District Courts regarding 26 CFR matters, Civil Jurisdiction.

70. The use of Book 68A sections which attach to 27 CFR, claiming they attach to 26 CFR issues is a clear violation of 18 USC 241.

71. The IRS making a Return of Information document to the USDJ to attempt illegal prosecution of a Citizen for a 26 CFR offense (of which there are none) **knowingly falsely** using IRC sections (the Book 68A) which can only be used for 27 CFR issues **is a Felony,** violating **18 USC 241: Conspiracy against citizen rights, 18 USC 1018: False writings and fraud,** and **18 USC Chapter 73: Obstruction of Justice,** and Executive Order 12630 March 15, 1988.

72. No treasury Order gives authority to the IRS to conduct investigations, secure "evidence" by fraud, conduct searches and seizures, or make a Return of Information Complaint to the USDJ.

73. The US District Courts cannot by Case Law make Statute Law, where Statute Law does not exist, nor can the Courts give themselves Jurisdiction where the Legislative body (Congress) by Public Law has not given them specific Subject Matter Jurisdiction; 28 USC section 1340 confers only Civil Jurisdiction for 26 CFR.

Maine Republic Email Alert

No.087

"... that I should bear witness unto the truth." — *John 18:33* // *David E. Robinson, Publisher*

"... if the trumpet give an uncertain sound, who shall prepare himself for battle?" — *I Corinthians 14:8* — 05/04/12

The Internal Revenue is not the Internal Revenue Service

The **Internal Revenue** of the United States government, is not the **Internal Revenue Service** of the Federal Reserve Bank.

The **Internal Revenue** determines tax debts for the United States, while the **Internal Revenue Service** collects those tax debts for the Federal Reserve Bank.

It's all about the "bill" and not the "law".

Use Title 15 for your defense, instead of Title 26 and the Constitution. Title 15 relates to "verified Assessment". The collector must provide **proof of the debt** to validate the debt. Any case involving debt must be held in a judicial district court.

The IRS circumvents the Constitution by using **their** tax law *(Title 26)* to confuse their victims.

Tax law doesn't apply. The IRS is a **debt collection agency** of the non-federal Federal Reserve Bank. Thus, the IRS is required to follow Title 15 of the United States Code.

What's more, the IRS has no way to verify the debt — unless you voluntarily assess *yourself* for an "income" debt that you do not owe.

The IRS, by its corporate charter and its own admission, is a debt collection agency. Debt collection agencies are subject to Title 15 of the United States Code — not to USC Title 26.

It seems that the primary strategy of the IRS is to get us to fight the wrong battle — to play the wrong game in the wrong court.

Although Title 26 is the Internal Revenue Code— the Code of the Internal Revenue, — the IRS is a collection agency of the Federal Reserve Bank and collection agencies must follow Title 15.

If you don't demand that the IRS verify the debt, then you are agreeing that the IRS' "bill" is valid. In other words, you are voluntarily condemning yourself to an "income" tax that you do not otherwise owe.

This is no different that a court officer tricking you into fighting an *accusation,* when you should be fighting the *charge.*

So what is the Remedy for this case?

Title 15 > Chapter 41 > Subchapter V > **Section 1692**

§ 1692. Congressional findings and declaration of purpose.

(a) Abusive practices

[*The invasion of individual privacy is an abusive, deceptive, and unfair debt collection practice.*]

(e) Purposes

[*It is the purpose of this sub-chapter...to protect* consumers *against debt collection abuses.*]

§ 1692a. Definitions

(5) [*The term "debt" means any obligation...whether or not such obliga-tion has been* reduced to judgment.]

§ 1692b. Acquisition of location information. Any debt collector...shall

(1) The false representation or implication that the debt collector is vouched for, bonded by, or affiliated with the United States or any State, including the use of any badge, uniform, or facsimile thereof.

HERE'S THE SILVER BULLET

Title 26 USC has nothing to do with the INTERNAL REVENUE SERVICE, it only applies to the INTERNAL REVENUE.

The giveaway is in Title 26, section 7802(b)(1)(c)

7802 INTERNAL REVENUE SERVICE OVERSIGHT BOARD

(b)(1)(c) one member shall be the Commissioner of the Internal Revenue.

Hence, "The Internal Revenue Code" is not "The Internal Revenue Service Code".

The "Internal Revenue" and the Internal Revenue Service" are two separate and distinct entities.

The "Internal Revenue" is a govern-ment agency under the scope of Title 26.

The "Internal Revenue Service" us a private for profit corporation under the scope of Title 15.

If you look up Internal Revenue Service in the Index of Title 26 you will discover that it is only mentioned in a few sections. None of which have anything to do with determining the tax, they only deal with governance, collection and the like.

UNDISPUTED CONCLUSIONS

Title 15 > Chapter 41 > Sub-chapter V > Section 1692 is and act of Congress designed to protect *natural persons.*

1692a. The term *"consumer"* means any *natural person* obligated or allegedly obligated to pay any debt.

THE INTERNAL REVENUE SERVICE is not part of the United States Government. See: *Diversified Metal Products v. T-Bow Co. Trust/ IRS 93-405-E-EJL.*

THE INTERNAL REVENUE SERVICE is incorporated in Delaware **as a collection agency for a Puerto Rico company; INTERNAL REVENUE TAX AND AUDIT SERVICE (IRS)** For Profit General Delaware Corporation. Incorporation Date 7/12/33, File No. 0325720.

Several Corporations involved with the INTERNAL REVENUE SERVICE are also unlawfully acting under color of law as government agencies, as well.

Consider adding the word "Service" to other entities and see how it works.

FEDERAL RESERVE ASSOCIA-TION (Federal Reserve) Non-profit Delaware Corporation. Incorporation Date 9/13/14 File No. 0042817

CENTRAL INTELLIGENCE AUTHORITY INC. (CIA) Non-profit Delaware Corporation. Incorporation Date 3/9/83 File No. 2004409

UNITED STATES OF AMERICA, INC. Non-profit Delaware Corporation. Incorporation Date 4/19/89 File No. 2193946

FEDERAL LAND ACQUISITION CORP. For-profit Delaware Corporation. Incorporation Date 8/22/80. File No. 0897960

RTC COMMERCIAL ASSETS TRUST 1995-NP3-2. For-profit Delaware Corporation. Incorporation Date 10/24/95. File No. 2554768

SOCIAL SECURITY CORP., DEPT. OF HEALTH, EDUCATION AND WELFARE. For-profit Delaware Statutory Trust. Incorporation Date 11/13/89. File No. 2213135

"ad Christi potentium et gloriam"
(for the power and glory of Christ)

Maine Republic Email Alert

No.088

"... that I should bear witness unto the truth." — John 18:33 // David E. Robinson, Publisher

"... if the trumpet give an uncertain sound, who shall prepare himself for battle?" — I Corinthians 14:8 —   05/04/12

Nil-Dicit Judgment (*"he says nothing" judgment*)

The first rule of winning in court is to win before going to court. **The second rule** is to make the other party argue about something other than the case. IRS attorneys know this, so we should know this too.

The IRS is a debt collection service.

When the IRS charges someone with willful failure to file under civil law they are actually *billing the victim* for a tax. The victim then tries to fight the IRS using the Constitution and/or Title 26 of the United States Code without ever asking for a *verified assessment* of the debt under Title 15.

This *lack of request* gives the IRS the ability to obtain a *nil-dicit judgment* against the victim in UNITED STATES DISTRICT COURT, making the bill a lawful bill.

Once the bill is deemed lawful, the IRS gets to claim that the victim is fraudulently refusing to pay a legal debt, and converts the refusal to pay into some kind of criminal act.

Whereas in reality, since the IRS is a debt collection service for the non-federal Federal Reserve Bank, the victim can require that the IRS verify the assessment, *which the IRS cannot do,* — and if it could, the victim could make the IRS take the action to the jurisdictional district the alleged debtor is in.

However the IRS cannot verify the alleged debt assessment; only the victim can do that by admitting the claim.

Going to court and arguing about taxes using Title 26 is ineffective for the following reasons:

1. Title 26 is used by the government to *determine* the tax.

2. The IRS is a debt collection service, not a government agency. *see Diversified Metal v. T-Bow Trust/IRS*

3. The bill issued by the U.S. Treasury *(under Title 26)* becomes a debt collectable by the IRS *(which has to follow Title 15).*

4. If you fight the IRS under Title 26, you are fighting something they have nothing to do with. It's like contesting the electric bill to the mail man, he will just think you are a nag, and he can't do anything about it anyhow.

5. The bill has already been adjudicated under *nil-dicit judgment* and stands *if not contested under Title 15. You cannot contest the bill under Title 26 since that is the government code on how to figure the bill, not the bill itself.*

6. Demanding that the IRS verify the assessment *(the bill)* requires them to cease and desist *(under Title 15)* until they supply the documents.

7. The IRS cannot supply the requisite documents and therefore you have beat them before going to court. *see Rule 1.*

8. If you go to court you can argue the correct issue, *the bill,* not how they *determined* the bill, thusly you can win by arguing the right argument. *rule 2.*

9. You can force the IRS to do the action in the judicial district, *i.e. the court nearest the debtor,* which they will not do, and therefore you won't go to court. *see YHWH's scriptures.*

Title 26 > Subtitle F > Chapter 76 > Subchapter A > Section 7408

§ 7408. *Actions to enjoin specified conduct related to tax shelters and reportable transactions.*

(d) Citizens and residents outside the United States

If any citizen or resident of the United States does not reside in, and does not have his principal place of business in, any United States judicial district, such citizen or resident shall be treated for purposes of this section as residing in the District of Columbia.

One of the common denominators of acquittals is that somewhere or somehow the victim did some type of request for assessment that was never affirmed.

This is diametrically opposite to all the victims who lost using Title 26 and the absence of applicability to the code.

In summary, just like a charge in a traffic ticket, don't fight the law and *their* reasoning, deny the bill and require them to prove that the bill exists as a matter of record, before they *make* it a matter of record under *nil-dicit judgment* because you didn't deny it.

Example:
A contractor (government under Title 26) issues you (contractee) a bill through their third party collection service (IRS), you do not respond. Third party collector service, whose actions and remedies are defined in Title 15, goes to court ex-parte and receives a nil-dicit judgment. You get dragged into a foreign court (USDC) and attempt to fight the contractor and their rules for issuing the bill under the Constitution and/or Title 26, neither of which applies, since it is the bill being discussed, not the entity that issued the bill or how said entity determined the amount. Any attorney would tell you that this is a waste of time. You (contractee) must first void the bill under the appropriate code (Title 15) and demand the case be kept in the proper jurisdiction (the nearest judicial district).

In essence, Title 26 applies to the government entity that determined the bill and Title 15 applies to the collection agency attacking you for payment.

Title 26, THE IRC has little to do with the IRS.

Maine Republic Email Alert

No.090

". . . that I should bear witness unto the truth." — John 18:33 // David E. Robinson, Publisher

". . . if the trumpet give an uncertain sound, who shall prepare himself for battle?" — I Corinthians 14:8 —   *05/08/12*

IRS Levys and Liens

Written By - Rico S. Giron, Future Sheriff of San Miguel County, New Mexico. http://ricoforsheriff.com

The Federal Reserve Bank, a.k.a. the IRS, is the biggest lie and scam in world history.

I.R.S. - are the three most frightening and loathed letters in the English language.

This deep-seated fear and loathing serves a very specific purpose. It serves to keep the People of America enslaved in submission to an illusion, a lie. It is an emotional and psychological chain around the neck of the American people.

The IRS has a horrible reputation and has earned every bit of it, it has by their own admissions committed crimes against innocent Citizens, and continues to be the **"Gestapo" of America** today.

They confiscate more homes, destroy more families, take more money, ruin more lives, and commit more crimes than all the street gangs combined.

They are indeed vivid proof that *"The greatest threat we face as a nation is our own Federal Government!"* — from "The County Sheriff: America's Last Hope", by author Richard Mack.

Here it is in a nutshell:

The IRS is a private, debt collection agency for the private banking system known as the Federal Reserve Bank.

The IRS is not a government agency. I repeat, the IRS is not a government agency. Never has been, never will be.

The IRS is formerly the Bureau of Internal Revenue (BIR) situated in, and with authority only in, the Philippine Islands (Trust Fund # 61); moved into Puerto Rico (Trust Fund # 62).

In the 1950's, with the stroke of the pen, the BIR was transformed into the current, notorious IRS and brought onto the 50 united States.

This was done without any Congressional authority whatsoever. There is no Congressional authority for the IRS to exist and operate in the 50 states of the Union recorded anywhere in any law-books.

Again, keep in mind, that the IRS is the **"Private, debt collection agency for the private banking system known as the Federal Reserve Bank(s)".**

Due to the naive ignorance of the American people, most Americans do not realize that there are two titles 26.

Title 26, Internal Revenue Code, is the "Debt Collection Manual" for the IRS.

This manual has nothing with Constitutional Rights. The IRS does not collect an "income tax". The IRS is simply collecting a "user fee" payable to the Federal Reserve Bank because we Americans are using a *private credit system.* The user fee had to be disguised as an "income tax" to fool the American people and keep them enslaved.

Title 26, United States Code, is "non-positive" law, which means that no "American Citizen" is subject to it. However, all "U.S. citizens" *are* subject to it. In order to understand "U.S. citizen" you must go to 28 USC, section 3002.

Most "American Citizens" have perhaps *unknowingly,* but *voluntarily,* surrendered their Sovereignty in exchange for the "immunities and privileges" of the 14th Amendment.

There are literally hundreds of unilateral, silent contracts by which American Citizens *declare themselves* to be "U.S. citizens" and thus subject to *both* Titles 26.

By *voluntarily* becoming a "U.S. citizen", every "American Citizen" declares him/herself to be an "indentured servant" (a slave) to the non-federal, Federal Reserve Banking system with no Constitutional Rights whatsoever.

So then, Title 26, USC, is a *private law* that applies only to "U.S. corporate 'citizens'", who are **all** employees of the corporate entity identified at 28 USC, section 3002(15)(A)(B)(C).

(15) "United States" means—

(A) a Federal corporation;

(B) an agency, department, com-mission, board, or other entity of the United States; or

(C) an instrumentality of the United States.

Consider this fact.

When an IRS agent wants to seize property from a Citizen in a County, they must first contact the Sheriff of the County and request assistance in the seizure because the IRS agent has no authority to seize any property at all.

So the IRS agent bamboozles the Sheriff into committing the crime, **for the IRS.**

When the Sheriff seizes property from a Citizen under the *non-authority* of the IRS agent, the Sheriff has committed a Second Degree Felony, **Conversion of Property.**

A second degree felony is incredibly serious!

However, both the IRS agent and the Sheriff, knowingly or unknowingly, count on the ignorance of the Citizen who has no idea what their Lawful Rights are.

Bear this point in mind: If the IRS agent has no authority to seize any property at all, then they cannot *delegate,* or *confer* to the Sheriff what they themselves do not have.

In addition, the Sheriff has no idea that he has engaged in a serious crime.

Here is where the maxim, **"Ignorance of the law is no excuse** [for violating the law]" applies. Hence the maxim, **"The Law leaves the wrong-doer where it finds him".**

We do not have an excuse based on

"ad Christi potentium et gloriam"
(for the power and glory of Christ)

IRS Strategy

The IRS operates a clearly defined and very clever scam. Here is how it works.

(1) The IRS presumes a fictional, fraudulent, nebulous, libelous and imaginary assessment against a citizen.

(2) The IRS presents this assessment as a Notice of Tax Lien to the County Recorder.

(3) A Notice of Tax Lien is supposed to instruct the tax "debtor" as to where the actual Tax Lien can be found, studied, and copied so that it can be challenged if necessary, but the Notice of Tax Lien never does provide that information because the IRS never produces any Tax Liens to which a Notice could refer.

(4) An unlawful statute injected into the Revised Code of Washington at RCW 60.68.045 by the IRS, and uncritically allowed to reside there by legislators, other officers of the government, and citizens, directs the County Recorder to enter the "Notice of Tax Lien" on a "Tax Lien" Index.

(5) But a "Notice of Tax Lien" does not contain a sworn (affidavit) assessment and is therefore only a non-negotiable/non-"spendable" paper instrument, which means that it cannot be used as money after maturing unchallenged 90 days, to procure, seize and sell property.

(6) And a Lien, any lien, if lawfully constructed must contain a sworn (affidavit) assessment as part of the full disclosure requirement of all negotiable instruments, and is therefore a negotiable/"spendable" paper instrument, which means that it can be used as money after maturing unchallenged for 90 days, to procure, seize and sell property.

(7) Since the IRS never presents a Tax Lien to the County Recorder, because IRS agents do not want the liability for presenting a false, fraudulent, nebulous, and/or libelous assessment, it must procure *or suborn* the County Recorder to do IRS counterfeiting for it by counterfeiting the *appearance* of the existence of a Tax Lien by *changing* the title from a Notice into a Lien by unlawfully entering it on the wrong Index, a Tax Lien Index.

(8) By changing the title from a Notice into a Lien, the County Recorder has converted a non-negotiable/non-"spendable" paper into a negotiable/"spendable" ledger entry, and has therefore *counterfeited a currency,* for the IRS, lacking full disclosure.

(9) Then, all the IRS has to do is to ask the County Recorder for a Certified Copy of the **Tax Lien Index** to "prove" that a Lien has been filed. This Certified Copy of the **Tax Lien Index** has the same power in commerce as a Federal Reserve Note because it can be used as money to procure, seize and sell property, to transfer property from the citizens to the IRS.

(10) Once the IRS has the Certified Copy of the **Tax Lien Index** implying the filing of a Lien, the IRS can begin taking wages, bank accounts, investments, social security payments, retirement benefits, houses, cars, and just about anything else that will bring cash to the IRS directly or by auction.

(11) The Public, the Legal Establishment, and the Courts, are all conditioned by threats of IRS retaliation to do whatever the IRS dictates, so the scam is complete. Therefore, there is no remedy through the judicial courts.

The ONLY REMEDY of this problem is to ignore the judicial system and to use the same ancient and timeless system of commerce which the IRS uses, but to use the commercial system lawfully and properly by doing everything with **sworn affidavits containing full disclosure** (Exodus 20:16).

"ad Christi potentium et gloriam"
(for the power and glory of Christ)

Internal Revenue Service Personnel

Internal Revenue Service Personnel have no authority whatever to levy salaries and wages from privately owned companies.

IRS authority is applicable solely to **government agencies and personnel** by 26 U.S.C. 6331(a): "Levy may be made upon the accrued salary or wages of any officer, employee, or elected official, of the United States, the District of Columbia, or any agency or instrumentality of the United States or the District of Columbia, by serving a **notice of levy on the employer.**"

First, such notices must include a **Form 668B,** which is the actual levy.

Second, only those large businesses and governmental units that have designated officers and written agreements are authorized to receive notices of levy by mail.

Third, to complete the levy, another form, **Form 668C,** must be served, but cannot be served by mail; it must be served in person. That completes **service of "notice of levy".**

Absent **Form 668B** there is no evidence that there is a levy. In the event the IRS fails to serve **either or both the levy and Form 668C,** service of process is incomplete and the IRS defaults.

In brief, **there can be no seizure before a judgment in a state court is rendered.**

Further, the AGO (Attorney General's Office) states clearly that there are **two forms of judicial process** referred to above, **writs of attachment** and **writs of garnishment**.

Since **a notice of levy is neither,** it should be obvious that it is not **"service of process"** in any legal sense whatsoever. **Federal law says that a levy is served with a writ of attachment.** Writs of attachment have a different purpose than writs of garnishment.

A levy is not a garnishment; a levy is an <u>attachment</u>.

It takes a court action to compel anyone to surrender a consumer's property to another (such as the IRS) without the consumer's consent and over the consumers objection.

In sum, a "<u>notice of levy</u>" is not a levy nor a garnishment.

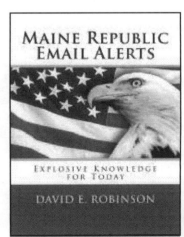

Maine Republic Email Alert

No.171

". . . that I should bear witness unto the truth." — John 18:33 // David E. Robinson, Publisher

". . . if the trumpet give an uncertain sound, who shall prepare himself for battle?" — I Corinthians 14:8 —   07/18/12

The IRS - The Biggest Lie

Posted by F. William Messier, of Brunswick, Maine:

THIS WAS WRITTEN BY A CANDIDATE FOR SHERIFF'S OFFICE IN SAN MATEO COUNTY, CALIFORNIA

IRS Liens and Levies

IRS-The biggest worst deal in World History

IRS-probably the three most frightening letters in the English language. This deep-seated fear and loathing serves a very specific purpose. It serves to keep the People of America in submission to an illusion, a lie.

The IRS has a horrible reputation and has earned every bit of it, has by their own admissions committed crimes against innocent Citizens, and continues today to be the "Gestapo" of America.

They confiscate more homes, destroy more families, take more money, ruin more lives, and commit more crimes than all the street gangs in America combined.

They are indeed vivid proof that the greatest threat we face, as a nation, is our own Federal" Government." [The County Sheriff: America's Last Hope. Author Richard Mack].

Here it is in a nutshell. **The IRS is the "Private, debt collection agency for the private banking system known as the non-federal Federal Reserve Bank"**. The IRS is not a government agency. I repeat, the IRS is not a government agency. Never has been, never will be.

The IRS is formerly the Bureau of Internal Revenue (BIR) situated in and with authority only in the Philippine

Islands (Trust Fund # 61), and moved into Puerto Rico (Trust Fund # 62).

In the 1950's, with the stroke of a pen, the BIR was transformed into the current notorious IRS and brought onto the 50 united States. This was done without any Congressional authority whatsoever.

There is no Congressional authority for the IRS to exist and operate in the 50 states; recorded anywhere in any lawbooks. Again, keep in mind, that **the IRS is the "Private, debt collection agency for the private banking system known as the non-federal Federal Reserve Bank".**

Consider this fact. When an IRS agent wants to seize property from a Citizen in a County, **they must first contact the Sheriff of the County and request assistance in the seizure.** This is because the IRS agent has no authority to seize any property at all. So the IRS agent bamboozles the Sheriff into committing the crime *for the IRS*. When the Sheriff seizes property from a Citizen under the non-authority of the IRS agent, **the Sheriff has committed a Second Degree Felony; Conversion of Property.**

A second degree felony is incredibly serious. However, both the IRS agent counts on the abysmal ignorance of the Citizen who has no idea what his Lawful Rights are. Bear this point in mind, since the IRS agent has no authority to seize any property at all, then he cannot delegate or confer to the Sheriff what he himself does not have. In addition, **the Sheriff has no idea that he has engaged in a serious crime.**

Here is where the maxim applies, **"Ignorance of the law, is no excuse for violating the law."** Both the IRS

agent and the Sheriff are subject to arrest and should be charged with Conversion of property, a second degree felony.

Tyranny is defined as: **Dominance through threat of punishment and violence; oppressive rule; abusive government; cruelty and injustice.**

What better definition than this fits the abusive IRS.

America is using a private credit system wherein the medium of exchange are the Federal Reserve Notes that we call "Dollars". Hence, **the so-called "Income Tax" is nothing more than a disguised "User Fee" that Americans must pay to the non-federal Federal Reserve Bank for using their private credit system.** [research **Title 12 USC**].

The legal definition of "dollar" is **"a gold or silver coin of a specific weight and with specific markings".** Thus, a Federal Reserve Note, is not and cannot, ever be a dollar. **A Note is not "money"**, see Blacks Law Dictionary. The Federal Reserve Notes currently in use are mere evidence of a debt.

The Federal Reserve Banking system is not a Federal government agency; there are no "reserves" and there is no real money. The Federal Reserve Banking system is a private cartel that has usurped the authority of the Congress to coin Money.

Federal Reserve Notes are just as worthless or just as valuable as Monopoly Money used in the game "Monopoly".

If we go to **this** Constitution for the united States of America, Article I, section 8, we find that only Congress was given the authority **"To coin money, regulate the Value thereof, and of foreign Coin, and fix the Standard of Weights and Measures"**.

This authority given to Congress by **this** Constitution for the united States of America, was not to be delegated to any private corporation for that corporation's private gain.

("...**this** Constitution **for** the United States of America." [See PREAMBLE, and ARTICLE VI, clause 3] is **not** "THE CONSTITUTION **OF** THE UNITED STATES OF AMERICA" that is currently in use today.)

The authority to coin money was usurped by the unlawful enactment of the Federal Reserve Act of 1913. The Federal Reserve Act is a "private law" **passed by only four Congressmen after the Congressional session closed in December of 1913.** Congress can pass both private laws and public laws. Congress does not have to tell the American Citizens which law is private and which law is public. We are simply led to believe that all laws are public. This is propaganda and brainwashing at its best.

This was a silent coup d' e-tat wherein the American People became the slaves of the Federal Reserve Bank. The "Killing Blow", the coup de grace [pronounced gra] was delivered upon the American People by Franklin D. Roosevelt in 1933 by removing the Gold Standard from the American economy.

Since then, no American Citizen has actually paid for anything, we have just exchanged worthless Federal Reserved Notes for more worthless Federal Reserve Notes. **All we do is lease our property** from the "STATE OF NEW MEXICO", **we lease our cars, we lease our houses, WE OWN NOTHING.**

Since 1933 **no American has owned his property in Allodium. That is why the "STATE** [OF NEW MEXICO]" **can take our property for just about any reason, i.e Eminent domain, failure to pay so-called "property taxes", etc.**

For anyone who has ever dealt with a debt collection agency, you know how nasty, mean and dirty they can be. Now, take that nastiness, that meanness and dirtiness and multiply it one hundred fold, there you have the attitude of the IRS.

Let's continue down the Rabbit Hole. When an American Citizen gets into a dispute with the IRS, the IRS agent will not listen to any of your pleadings, your begging's or your excuses. Everything you do or say amounts to nothing with the IRS. If you dig in your heels and refuse to pay, the IRS starts sending you threatening letters with dire consequences for your non-cooperation.

If you still refuse to pay, the IRS will file a document called a **"Notice of Federal Tax Lien"** in the local County Clerk's office. This is a very deceptive document. Keep one thing in mind a "Notice" is not the "Lien" itself. The "Lien" is a totally separate and distinct document from the "Notice". **The County Clerk, through ignorance files the "Notice of Federal Tax Lien" as if it were an actual "Lien".** These are two separate and distinct documents. **The County Clerk never requests the actual "Lien" from the IRS agent.** If they were to request this document, the IRS agent would get very irate and threaten the County Clerk for their non-cooperation. Of course, **the actual "Lien" does not exist!**

There is one more lawful requirement that the County Clerk must comply with before they can file the **"Notice of Federal Tax Lien"** or the actual **"Lien"** itself.

The Federal Lien Registration Act requires "Certification" of the "Lien" itself. This would require that the IRS agent file **an Affidavit** wherein they identify themselves, and state under Oath **that there is an actual "Lien" on file based on an actual assessment on form 23C,** against the particular American Citizen. When the County Clerk **fails to verify "Certification"** they violate the lawful requirements of the Federal Lien Registration Act.

The IRS never files the actual

"Lien" because it does not exist! An actual "Lien" must be based on a lawful assessment on form 23C. In the entire history of the IRS, the IRS has never produced a form 23C showing an individual assessment against an American Citizen.

This so-called **"Notice of Federal Tax Lien"** is an act of **"Financial Terrorism"** because once this **"Notice"** is filed, *you become a pariah, a financial outcast, you are branded as unfit, you are no longer a "good slave", you are a rebel beyond the hope of redemption.* Your slave "Credit Rating" takes a nosedive. You are practically ruined financially.

Interestingly, **Section 803** of the so-called **PATRIOT ACT** defines terrorism as *"any act intended to coerce or threaten a civilian population".* So by the very definition of "Terrorism", the IRS is the largest, meanest, dirtiest, Terrorist Organization in the entire world.

If you are still not intimidated, **the IRS will file a "Notice of Levy" with the County Clerk, and send copies to your bank(s) and employer.** The County Clerk, through ignorance, **files the "Notice of Levy" as if it were an actual "Levy".** These are two separate and distinct documents.

Again, keep in mind, **a "Notice" is not a "Levy".** On this "Notice" alone, **the bank then hands over all of your money to the IRS and you cannot even pay your bills!** Your employer garnishes your paycheck, and again, *you are the slave of the Federal Reserve Bank.* Your Bank treats the "Notice of Levy" as if it were an actual "Levy". Your employer also treats the "Notice of Levy" as if it were an actual "Levy". The bank and your employer never request an actual copy of the "Levy" itself. **Of course, the actual "Levy" does not exist!**

Both the bank and your employer fail to verify several key pieces of information in dealing with the IRS agent.

First, they fail to ask for a copy of the IRS agent's driver's license to verify that in fact they are who they say they are. So that in case, the IRS agent has to be served with legal process, they can be located. **(all IRS agents have been given instructions to never provide this information to any one asking for it. Thus, the true identity of the IRS agent is never established.)** Pretty convenient, Huh!

Second, the bank and your employer fail to request a copy of the "Pocket Commission" from the IRS agent. **Every IRS agent is assigned a "Pocket Commission".** This "Pocket Commission" identifies the IRS agent's authority as to his/her actions. The most common "Pocket Commission" is what is called **"Administrative".** This is identified with a capital **"A"** on their identity card. This means that this IRS agent can shuffle paperwork all day, **but he/she does not have any "Enforcement" authority whatsoever.**

The other "Pocket Commission" is what is called **"Enforcement".** The word "Enforcement" might convey the message that this IRS agent actually has unlimited authority to **"Enforce"** something against American Citizens. That is not the case at all. They have an extremely limited scope of authority. In fact, **they cannot enforce anything against American Citizens, without a warrant from the court.**

Both the bank and your employer fail to request a copy of the "Pocket Commission" from the IRS agent in order to establish the authority of the IRS agent. **I am fairly confident that all agents that send out notices to banks and employers have an "Administrative Pocket Commission". Thus, both your bank and your employer steal your money and send it to the Terrorist Agency known as the IRS.**

Thirdly, the bank and your employer fail to request a copy of the actual assessment on form 23C. Again, **never in the history of this country has an American Citizen been assessed an Income Tax on a form 23C.** Without this so-called assessment on this specific form, form 23C, **there is no debt.** So the bank and your employer

fail to verify this alleged debt and thus, steal your money.

Fourth, the bank and your employer fail to request of copy of the **"Abstract of Court Judgment".** This document would show that you were actually sued by the IRS and **that you had your day in court.** The Seventh Amendment of the Bill of Rights of this Constitution for the united States of America guarantees you **the Right of Trial by Jury in any controversy where the amount shall exceed twenty dollars.** Of course, you were never sued and you never had your day in court. Thus, **your Due Process of Law Rights are totally violated and again,** and you are further enslaved to the Federal Reserve Bank.

So then, we come to the end of the Rabbit Hole. **You have never owed any money to the IRS!** The IRS is simply the enforcer, the debt collector for the Federal Reserve Banking System. However, because you are using a private credit system, wherein the medium of exchange are fancy pieces of paper called Federal Reserve Notes, **you allegedly owe the Federal Reserve Bank a fraudulent "user fee".**

By way of information, the IRS does not have a bank account wherein your tax payments are deposited. **All of your tax payments are deposited into the bank account of the Federal Reserve Bank in one region or another.**

The Federal Reserve Banks and the IRS constitute the single largest sting operation, the single largest fraud and the single largest swindle in the history of the World.

In order to keep this "Alice in Wonderland" illusion going, the so-called "government" developed an entire industry to support and perpetuate this fraud. **The tax preparation industry.** Tax preparers, accountants, so-called Certified Public Accountants, self proclaimed financial gurus advising about tax loopholes, etc., etc.

All the current paycheck garnishments in the entire country could be stopped by having your employer request

the above mentioned documents, to wit:

1. A copy of the **Driver's License** of the IRS agent

2. A copy of the **"Pocket Commission"** showing the authority of the IRS agent

3. A copy of the **assessment** shown on form 23C against the American Citizen

4. A copy of the **"Abstract of Court Judgment"** that verifies that you had a trial by jury.

As the elected Sheriff of San Miguel County, New Mexico, **I will provide educational classes to the County Clerk and the employers who are currently garnishing wages and paychecks to identify areas where they may have broken the law and unwittingly stolen their employees Federal Reserve Notes and thus committed "Conversion of Property", a second degree felony.**

Furthermore, **I will work closely with the County Clerk through education and knowledge so that the Clerk can stop breaking the law and committing financial terrorism against the Citizens of San Miguel County.**

When the Citizens of San Miguel County elect me as their new Sheriff in town, **I will ban the IRS from San Miguel County, and if I catch an IRS agent within the boundaries of the county, without my permission, I will arrest them for TRESPASSING**

Posted by: Bill Messier

Private Pilot K1MNW

"AOPA Member"

Maine Republic Email Alert
No.174

". . . that I should bear witness unto the truth." — John 18:33 // David E. Robinson, Publisher

". . . if the trumpet give an uncertain sound, who shall prepare himself for battle?" — I Corinthians 14:8 — 07/25/12

The Organic Act of 1871

1871, February 21: Congress Passed an "Act to Provide a Government for the District of Columbia", also known as the "Act of 1871".

With no constitutional authority to do so, Congress created a separate form of government for the District of Columbia, a ten mile square parcel of land (see, Acts of the Forty-first Congress," Section 34, Session III, chapters 61 and 62).

The act — passed when the country was weakened and financially depleted in the aftermath of the Civil War — was a strategic move by foreign bankers who were intent upon gaining a stranglehold on the coffers of America.

Congress cut a deal with the international bankers and incurred a DEBT to them because they were not about to lend money to a floundering nation without serious stipulations. So they devised a way to get their foot in the door of the United States.

The Act of 1871 formed a corporation called THE UNITED STATES.

The corporation, owned by foreign interests, moved in and shoved the original Constitution aside. With the Act of 1871, the organic Constitution was altered when the title was capitalized and the word "for" was changed to "of" in the title.

THE CONSTITUTION OF THE UNITED STATES OF AMERICA is the constitution of the incorporated UNITED STATES OF AMERICA. It operates in an economic capacity and is being used to fool the People into thinking that it governs the Republic. But it does not!

Capitalization is significant when one is referring to a legal document. This seemingly "minor" alteration has had a major impact on every subsequent generation of Americans.

What Congress did by passing the Act of 1871 was create an entirely new document, a constitution for the government of the District of Columbia, an INCORPORATED business.

This newly altered Act of 1871 Constitution was not intended to benefit the Republic. It benefits the corporation of THE UNITED STATES OF AMERICA and operates entirely outside the original organic Constitution.

Instead of having absolute and unalienable rights guaranteed under the organic Constitution, we the people now have "relative" rights, or privileges. One example is the Sovereign's right to travel, that has now been transformed (under corporate government policy) into a "privilege" that requires citizens to be licensed. (Passports)

In passing the Act of 1871 Congress committed TREASON against the People who were Sovereign under the grants and decrees of the Declaration of Independence and the organic Constitution.

The Act of 1871 became the FOUNDATION of all the treason committed by government officials ever since.

To fully understand how our rights of sovereignty were ended, you must understand the full meaning of the word sovereign: *"Chief or highest, supreme power, superior in position to all others; independent of and unlimited by others; possessing or entitled to; original and independent authority or jurisdiction."* (Webster).

In short, our government, which was created by and for us as sovereigns — *free citizens deemed to have the highest authority in the land* — was stolen from us, along with our rights. Keep in mind that, according to the original, organic

Constitution, We the People are sovereign; government is not sovereign. The Declaration of Independence says that **"government is subject to the consent of the governed"**; that's us. We're sovereigns. When did you last feel like a sovereign?

It doesn't take a rocket scientist or a constitutional historian to figure out that the U.S. Government has NOT been subject to the consent of the governed since long before you or I were born.

Rather, the governed are subject to the whim and greed of the corporation, which has stretched its tentacles beyond the ten-mile-square parcel of land known as the District of Columbia. It has invaded every state of the Republic.

However, the corporation has NO jurisdiction beyond the District of Columbia. You just think it does.

You are 'presumed' to know the law, but We the People are taught NOTHING about the law in school. We memorize obscure facts and phrases, here and there, like the Preamble, which says, *"We the People...establish this Constitution for the United States of America."* But our teachers only gloss over the Bill of Rights. Our schools, which are controlled by the corporate government, don't delve into the Constitution in depth.

The corporation was established to indoctrinate and 'dumb-down' the masses, not to teach anything of value or importance. Certainly, no one mentioned that America was "sold-out" to foreign interests, and that we were obligated to pay the debt incurred by Congress, or that we are in debt to the international bankers.

Yet, for generations, Americans have had the bulk of their earnings confiscated to pay a massive debt that they did not incur and do not owe.

There's an endless stream of things that the People aren't told. And, now that you are being told, how do you feel about being made the recipient of a debt without your knowledge or consent?

After passage of the Act of 1871 Congress set a series of subtle and overt deceptions into motion, deceptions in the form of decisions that were meant to sell us down the river. Over time, the Republic took it on the chin until it was knocked down and counted out by a technical KO [knock out].

With the surrender of the people's gold in 1933, the 'common herd' was placed under illegitimate law.

(I'll bet you weren't taught THIS in school.)

Our corporate form of government is based on Roman Civil Law and Admiralty or Maritime Law, which is also known as the "Divine Right of Kings" and the "Law of the Seas" — another fact of American history not taught in our schools.

Actually, Roman Civil Law was fully established in the colonies before our nation began, and then became managed by private international law. In other words, the government — the government created for the District of Columbia via the Act of 1871 – operates under Private International Law, not the Common Law foundation of our Constitutional Republic.

This fact has impacted all Americans in concrete ways. For instance, although Private International Law is technically only applicable within the District of Columbia, and NOT in the other states of the Union, the arms of the Corporation of THE UNITED STATES are called "departments": the Justice Department; the Treasury Department; etc. And these departments affect everyone, no matter where and in what state they live.

Each department belongs to the corporation — to THE UNITED STATES.

"Refer to any UNITED STATES CODE (USC). Note the capitalization; this is evidence of a corporation, not of a Republic. For example, In Title 28 3002 (15)(A)(B)(C), it is unequivocally stated that **the UNITED STATES is a corporation.**

Translation: the corporation is NOT a separate and distinct entity; it is not disconnected from the government; **it IS the government — your government.**

This is extremely important! I refer to it as the **"Corporate EMPIRE of the UNITED STATES"** which operates under Roman Civil Law outside the original Constitution. How do you like being ruled by a corporation?

You say you'll ask your Congressperson about this? "HA!! "

Congress is fully aware of this deception. So it's time that you, too, be aware of the deception. What this great deception means is that **the members of Congress do NOT work for us, for you and me. They work for the Corporation, for the UNITED STATES**. No wonder we can't get them to do anything on our behalf, or meet or demands, or answer our questions.

Technically, legally, or any other way you want to look at the matter, **the corporate government of the UNITED STATES has no jurisdiction or authority in ANY State of the Union (the Republic) beyond the District of Columbia.**

Let that tidbit sink in, then ask yourself, could this deception have occurred without the full knowledge and complicity of the Congress? Do you think it happened by accident? If you do, you're deceiving yourself.

There are no accidents, no coincidences. Face the facts and confront the truth. Remember, you are presumed to know the law. THEY know you don't know the law or, for that matter, your history. Why?

Because no concerted effort was ever made to teach or otherwise inform you. As a Sovereign, you are entitled to full disclosure of all facts. As a slave, you are entitled to nothing other than what the corporation decides to 'give' you.

Remember also that "Ignorance of the law is no excuse." It's your responsibility and obligation to learn the law and know how it applies to you. No wonder the Act of 1871 corporation counted on the fact that most people are too indifferent,

unconcerned, distracted, or lazy to learn what they need to know to survive within the system. We have been conditioned to let the government do our thinking for us. Now's the time to turn that around if we intend to help save our Republic and ourselves — before it's too late.

As an instrument of the international bankers, the UNITED STATES owns you from birth to death. It also holds ownership of all your assets, of your property, even of your children. Think long and hard about all the bills taxes, fines, and licenses you have paid for or purchased. Yes, they had you by the pockets.

If you don't believe it, read the 14th Amendment. See how "free" you really are. Ignorance of the facts led to your silence. **Silence is construed as consent;** consent to be obligated for a debt you did not incur. As a Sovereign People we have been deceived for hundreds of years; **we think we are free, but in truth we are servants of the corporation.**

Congress committed treason against the People in 1871. Honest men could have corrected the fraud and treason. But there weren't enough honest men to counteract the lust for money and power. We lost more freedom than we will ever know, thanks to corporate infiltration of our so-called "government".

Do you think that any soldier who died in any of our many wars would have fought if he or she had known the truth? Do you think one person would have laid down his/her life for a corporation? How long will we remain silent? How long will we perpetuate THE MYTH that we are free? When will we stand together as One Sovereign People? When will we take back what has been as stolen from the us?

If the People of America had known to what extent their trust has been betrayed, how long would it have taken for a real revolution to occur? What we now need is a Revolution in THOUGHT.

We need to change our thinking, then we can change our world. Our children deserve their rightful legacy — the liberty our ancestors fought to preserve, the legacy of a Sovereign and Fully Free People.

Maine Republic Email Alert

No.156

". . . that I should bear witness unto the truth." — John 18:33 // David E. Robinson, Publisher

". . . if the trumpet give an uncertain sound, who shall prepare himself for battle?" — I Corinthians 14:8 — 07/081/12

Maine Governor Paul LePage Speaks Out !

Gov. LePage calls IRS "new Gestapo" in his weekly radio address!

During his weekly radio address, Gov. Paul LePage reacted to the US Supreme Court's decision on the Affordable Health Care Act strongly, describing President Obama's health care reform in harsh terms and referring to the IRS as the "new Gestapo."

In arguing the court's decision made America less free, LePage said, "We the people have been told there is no choice. You must buy health insurance or pay the new Gestapo - the I.R.S." The governor also said he needs more information before deciding whether to expand the state's Medicaid program, a part of the law the court struck down, but the federal government would pay all of the cost for the expansion from 2014 to 2016 before reducing its support to 90 percent of the cost.

On Saturday, Maine Governor Paul LePage called the IRS the "new Gestapo" in his weekly radio address, the Portland Free Press reported.

"We the people have been told there is no choice," the Maine Republican said. "You must buy health insurance or pay the new Gestapo – the IRS."

Gov. LePage was referring to a provision in the health care law recently upheld by the Supreme Court that says Americans must either buy health insurance or face a stiff penalty. That provision, known as the individual mandate, is to be enforced by the Internal Revenue Service.

According to the Governor, the court

decision has "made America less free," and gives the government too much control over individual's lives.

According to the Governor, the court decision has "made America less free," and gives the government too much control over individual's lives.

"Perhaps what is most disturbing about this ruling, though, is that the federal mandate is considered a tax," he said. *"This tax will add to the $500 billion in tax increases that are already in Obamacare. Now that Congress can use the taxation power of the federal government to com*

A 2010 report at the Washington Examiner said the new taxes and mandates "will cause the greatest expansion of the Internal Revenue Service since World War II," with an estimated 16,500 new agents.

Maine Democrats did not care for Gov. LePage's characterization.

The Press Herald added:

Maine Democratic Party Chairman Ben Grant, responding to LePage's remarks, said, *"We've come to expect a bunch of nonsense from Gov. LePage, but this is a step too far. There appears now to be no limit to the extreme language he will use to misinform,* degrade and insult people. Somebody needs to explain to him that he's the governor of a state, and not a talk radio host. I demand a full apology on behalf of all those who suffered at the hands of the real Gestapo."

The feared Gestapo was the official secret police in Hitler's Germany, and was responsible for the deaths of thousands in the Third Reich.

Gov. LePage also said the state would not move forward on the healthcare exchanges, due to "looming uncertainties" over funding.

President Obama, he said, "has proposed $800 million to finance exchanges," but that money has not been approved by Congress.

"Government-run health care is not what the American dream is about," he added.

"America wasn't born on these sorts of principles and it's time we get back on track - not only for our future generations, but for the future of our Nation," he concluded.

"ad Christi potentium et gloriam"
(for the power and glory of Christ)

Maine Republic Email Alert

No.157

". . . that I should bear witness unto the truth." — John 18:33 // David E. Robinson, Publisher

". . . if the trumpet give an uncertain sound, who shall prepare himself for battle?" — I Corinthians 14:8 — 07/091/12

Request For Discovery !

DAVID E. ROBINSON, ELECTED ATTORNEY GENERAL FOR THE MAINE FREE STATE TRUST

3 Linnell Circle, Brunswick, Maine 04011

May 16, 2012

This **"Request for Discovery"** is in regard to the fraudulent IRS NOTICES OF LIEN being sent to you — Accounts Payable — by the IRS against F. WILLIAM MESSIER, 40 Tower Lane, Brunswick ME 04011.

DEAR ACCOUNTS PAYABLE,

The Federal Reserve is no more a federal agency than is Federal Express!

The Internal Revenue Service is no more a federal agency than is Dagget & Parker, or McDonalds!

The "Internal Revenue Service" is incorporated in Delaware as a "collection agency" for a Puerto Rican Company titled "Internal Revenue Tax & Audit Service" (IRS) — a for-profit corporation — Incorporated on 07/12/33 — File No. 0325720.

Therefore the "Internal Revenue Service" must be recognized in its lawful status as a "DEBT COLLECTION AGENCY" [under Title 15 instead of Title 26] and not be fraudulently accepted as a [U.S.] "Government Agency".

A "Notice of Levy" is not a "Levy"! — In dealing with an IRS "debt collector" Agent (or any other "debt collector") the following Seven items of information need to be obtained for "Proof of Claim".

(1) Ask the IRS Agent for a copy of his "DRIVER'S LICENSE" to verify that he is who he says he is. You need to record the "License Number" for possible use in case he has to be served with legal papers, so he can be located for proper service.

Gov. LePage calls IRS "new Gestapo" in his weekly radio address!

During his weekly radio address, Gov. Paul LePage reacted to the US Supreme Court's decision on the Affordable Health Care Act strongly, describing President Obama's health care reform in harsh terms and referring to the IRS as the "new Gestapo." In arguing the court's decision made America less free, LePage said, "We the people have been told there is no choice. You must buy health insurance or pay the new Gestapo - the I.R.S." The governor also said he needs more information before deciding whether to expand the state's Medicaid program, a part of the law the court struck down, but the federal government would pay all of the cost for the expansion from 2014 to 2016 before reducing its support to 90 percent of the cost.

(2) Ask the IRS Agent for a copy of his "POCKET COMMISSION MANUAL" showing his "authority to act" in this case. The most common type is "Administrator" (type A). The second type is "Enforcer" (type E). Administrators can only shuffle the paperwork. They cannot enforce the IRS law.

(3) Ask the IRS Agent for a copy of the "ACTUAL ASSESSMENT" — NOT the 668-A Notice of Levy — showing what the IRS claims the alleged "taxpayer" owes — according to the Internal Revenue, that the Internal Revenue Service is authorized to collect.

(4) Ask the IRS Agent for a copy of the "ABSTRACT OF COURT JUDGMENT" that verifies that the alleged "taxpayer" has a Jury Trial before any of his assets could be seized.

(5) Demand that the IRS Agent confirm all of his written answers under the penalty of perjury.

(6) Demand that the IRS Agent provide you with a copy of the "missing part (a)" (of Section 6331 "Levy and Distraint") missing on the back of the 668-A "Notice of Levy".

(7) Ask the IRS Agent which "Title" he is operating under — Title 26 of the "IR Code" or Title 15 of the "US Code" regarding corporations.

The Internal Revenue (IR) is a government agency under Title 26 of the "IR Code" Manual.

The Internal Revenue Service (IRS) is a private foreign for-profit "debt-collection agency" — it is not connected with any government — it operates under Title 15 of the "US Code".

By sending Mr. F. William Messier's Property (his money) to the IRS without judicial process of law and without first having verified the AUTHENTICITY of the

IRS Agent's claims, you may be liable

to PROSECUTION for having committed illegal "CONVERSION OF PROPERTY" — which is a second degree felony punishable by a fine and/or imprisonment or both.

Debt-collection agencies are subject to Title 15 of the United States Code relating to "Verified Assessment" whereby the "Debt Collection Agency" (of which you are now a debt-collector extension) must provide "proof of the claim" to validate the debt.

Any case involving the collection of debt must have been adjudicated in a local judicial district court.

The IRS has no way to verify an alleged debt without the alleged "taxpayer" voluntarily assessing himself.

According to Title 15, Section 1692, a debt-collector...

1. must legally identify himself;

2. must not state that the consumer owes any debt;

3. must not use any symbol that indicates that he is in the debt-collection business;

4. must not imply that he is affiliated with the United States Government or any of the states.

It is obvious that the IRS Agent has NOT obeyed these legal requirements in this case.

Please acknowledge the receipt of this letter by sending an email from a company contact to:

F. William Messier--
k1mnw@yahoo.com

David E. Robinson --
drobin88@comcast.net

Obtain Copies of the (7) Items of Verification listed above from IRS "DEBT-COLLECTION AGENT" JOLINE P. HENDERSHOT, 217 MAIN STREET, LEWISTON ME 04240, and from IRS "DEBT-COLLECTION AGENT" PATRICK FRIE, 220 MAINE MALL ROAD, SOUTH PORTLAND ME 04106.

Send duplicate copies, and copies of all correspondence sent to you from the IRS, to me by snail mail, to the above letterhead-address, within the next twenty (20) days from your receipt of this Demand. More time will be granted upon your written request. Failure to timely comply will be taken as material evidence that you refuse to honor this Demand.

I await your timely response.

Sincerely,

David E. Robinson
Interim Attorney General
for the Maine Free State Trust

Attached:

Maine Republic Email Newsletter Alerts:

#087 The Internal Revenue is not the Internal Revenue Service

#088 Nil-dicit Judgment ("he says nothing" judgment)

#090 IRS Levis and Liens

#094 IRS Strategy

#095 Internal Revenue Service Personnel

- X - X - X - X - X - X - X- X - X - X - X - X - X - X- X - X - X - X - X - X - X - X - X - X - X - X - X - X - X - X - X - X - X -

DISCLAIMER

Please note that the court system in America is an adversarial dual between a challenged party and a respondent party adversarially fought with ideas, concepts, and words instead of with the weapons of war, therefore in this report, names have not been removed to protect those who are alleged to be guilty. In this New World Order of intimate surveillance that we have naively allowed to take place the "third eye" above the pyramid of illuminati power is ever watching the sovereign people of America for the evil purpose of keeping all Americans dumbed down and enslaved. Note that <u>AS MAINE GOES SO GOES THE NATION!</u>

http://americannationalmilitia.com/
http://americannationalmilitia.com/2012/07/notice-to-the-world-was-delivered-to-the-office-of-private-international-law-at-the-hague/
http://americannationalmilitia.com/wp-content/uploads/2012/07/148-NOTICE-to-the-world.pdf

Maine Republic Email Alert

No.166

". . . that I should bear witness unto the truth." — John 18:33 // David E. Robinson, Publisher

". . . if the trumpet give an uncertain sound, who shall prepare himself for battle?" — I Corinthians 14:8 —   07/16/12

Layers of Conspiracy

By Cobra:

At the core of the physical Cabal there is a group of 13 Archons that has been controlling our planet for the last 26,000 years. They are responsible for the fall of Atlantis, for the collapse of peaceful Goddess worshipping neolithic cultures 5000 years ago, and for the destruction of the mystery schools in late antiquity. They are the ones that maintained the quarantine and kept humanity hostage so that the positive ETs could not intervene until now. They are mostly incarnated into key positions inside the Italian black nobility.

Their leader was arrested in Rome on May 5th, 2012, removed from this planet, and taken immediately to the Galactic Central Sun. He was the one that many members of the Cabal were worshipping in their distorted rituals, so now they are worshipping something that does not exist any longer.

About 2500 years ago, the Archons created a special task group and infiltrated it into the Ptolemaic dynasty in Egypt:

http://tinyurl.com/cc4hb72

This task group was responsible for the mind programming and mass control of humanity through organized religions during the last 2500 years. After the death of Cleopatra, their power was transferred from the Ptolemaic bloodline towards the Julio-Claudean dynasty in Rome, then to the Flavians, then to the Constantinian dynasty, then to the Theodosian dynasty and then to the Byzantine Giustiniani family. After the middle ages, members of this group incarnated mostly into positions of power within the Italian black nobility families. The Resistance took strong actions against this group in 2010 and it lost much of its power then.

This group created the Jesuits and the Jesuits have been running the show on this planet for the last 500 years, as you can read in this fairly accurate, although somewhat outdated report:

http://www.whale.to/b/pope.html

http://tinyurl.com/cf7e43a

Hans Kolvenbach is the old black Pope, the new one is Adolfo Nicolas.

This is how the Jesuits run the USA corporation:

http://tinyurl.com/cr3puwx

The Rothschilds have been the bankers for the Jesuits during the last two centuries. The most influential are: Jacob de Rothschild, Evelyn de Rothschild, David de Rothschild and lately also Nathaniel Philip de Rothschild.

The Rockefeller-Illuminazi faction is a Jesuit creation of the 20th century with a purpose to hinder and misuse the technological and scientific progress of humanity:

http://tinyurl.com/cbum6tj

The key players of the Rockefeller-Illuminazi faction are: David Rockefeller, Henry Kissinger, George Herbert Walker Bush (George Scherf Jr.), Dick Cheney, Jay Rockefeller, Donald Rumsfeld, Karl Rove and Paul Wolfowitz.

"ad Christi potentium et gloriam"
(for the power and glory of Christ)

Maine Republic Email Alert

No.247

". . . that I should bear witness unto the truth." — John 18:33 // David E. Robinson, Publisher

". . . if the trumpet give an uncertain sound, who shall prepare himself for battle?" — I Corinthians 14:8 —   *09/22/12*

Major Changes Ahead !

We are in a time of great change. **America's *Currency* was captured in 1913, and America's *Government* was captured in 1933.** This explains why petitioning our government for grievances has been to no meaningful avail.

Corporations that masquerade as our lawful government today, have almost *destroyed* America! Top people in our government — *including our military* — know this. They have been waiting for the "right time" to help *take America back to our lawful government.*

In the very near future, we can expect a major constructive change in our banking and currency system. We can expect to see contingents of Federal Marshals acting in the major seats of power — backed up by our Military.

These Military people are NOT any part of a military coup. They are backing up the Civilian re-establishment of our lost, lawful, government.

We can expect to see minor interruptions in our normal way of life.

This Transition has been designed to minimize interruptions in vital services in our economy — to minimize hardship.

This Transition will be accompanied by announcements in mainstream media. What we do *not* want is for people to become alarmed.

Our *so-called* "president" has been informed that he is *no longer* the Commander in Chief of our Military!

This is part of a worldwide operation whereby the non-aligned nations — *those nations that are not part of the G20* — will re-establish solid currencies.

There will be additional announcements to come — designed to slowly awaken the masses; to reduce panic.

Civil authority has been restored to the people. The Military, who exist only through Civil authority, will be ready to assist the People whom they are sworn to protect in the effort to restore this nation to the Constitutional Republic it was created to be.

International Law has been unlawfully in effect in America since 1933. And *rescinding this law,* has been on the table since the 1950s.

We the People have regained Civilian Authority, in order to use the Military Services to support the ongoing effort to bring us back to true government *"of, for and by the people".*

Do *not* misread what is going on — they are *NOT* coming for the People. **The Cabal's time is up!**

Please prepare for *"good"* changes to come.

Please share this information with others. The foundation has been laid. All that is needed now is YOU! — regular, everyday people will be needed for their insight, opinions and voice.

PLEASE SHARE THIS INFORMATION; EVERY AMERICAN MUST HEAR THIS, TO KNOW WHAT IS HAPPENING!

UFO Disclosure
http://tinyurl.com/c2pbsxn

"ad Christi potentium et gloriam"
(for the power and glory of Christ)

Maine Republic Email Alert

No.246

". . . that I should bear witness unto the truth." — John 18:33 // David E. Robinson, Publisher

". . . if the trumpet give an uncertain sound, who shall prepare himself for battle?" — I Corinthians 14:8 —   09/20/12

Disclosure is about to take place, re. Notice to the world

Just before the end of last year, Pennsylvania — *as a state* — put together a **Declaration of Notice to the world** stating that the Commonwealth of Pennsylvania had returned itself and its people back under its *de jur* Constitution, *of the 1700s,* and declared the People of Pennsylvania, Free! — no longer recognizing *unlawful corporate government* within their state.

They did this *legally and properly.* They did not ask for permission, they simply went ahead and did it. And they received their shipping receipt back from the **Office of Private International Law at the Hague.**

Shortly after that, an informed contact — who had been in touch with various groups who had come forward about that time — was contacted and given a simple message, and that message was this:

"It has come to our attention, what Pennsylvania has done. How long would it take you to put together a simple majority of states to duplicate what Pennsylvania has done, for at such a time there could be monetary and military support?"

They asked for a copy of the original documentation that Pennsylvania had submitted to the **Office of Private International Law at the Hague**, *so they could see who had been involved.*

Our confidential contact had no problem with that, and neither did Pennsylvania. So they forwarded to the contact the documentation that Pennsylvania had submitted.

The answer was *"Yes! we'll just see how fast we can get 'er done!"*

So they sent out emails to everyone across the country that they knew, and had worked with all this time, that they knew to be capable, honorable, and

honest Patriots, who would roll up their sleeves and actually get the job done, once they were told what had to be done.

And by the following day, at least one contact in 20-22 states had stepped up and volunteered to be a lead person in their state, to get 'er done!

The goal was for at least a simple majority — meaning 26 or more states to duplicate *exactly* what Pennsylvania had done.

It was later decided by those involved, to add *more strength* to the action by making the **Declaration of Notice to the world**, collectively as a united effort, so that the world will know we are not just free people in the various free states, but a Free People, *united as we were meant to be.*

We need no permission, recognition or opinion from foreign bodies or corporations to be what we are — **Americans who claim our rightful heritage that was given to us by our founders in 1776.**

This action should be seen as a *Declaration;* not just a notification — this is primary.

This action is interim; and we can't emphasize that enough.

A small group of elite people, have already messed things up — and in order to make sure that this doesn't happen again, all of the temporary aspects of this will be in writing.

After a period of about 120 days of "disclosure", free elections will be held. Paper ballots only; machines can be played with; paper ballots are a lot more difficult.

We've been told that old money people from before the Revolutionary War have been in contact with our military, and that some 80-90% of the military

agree with the ideology found in our founding documents.

Everything we do is based on the principles in our 1787 Constitution and the Bill of Rights — including the *original 13th Amendment* that prohibits any foreign association, title of nobility, etc. — and the Oath of Service that everybody must take to **"support and defend the Constitution of the United States against all enemies, foreign and domestic."**

The U.S. Military has indicated to the financial people that they are willing to back us and that we have their recognition and support.

This gives the Military — *probably for the first time* — power to be used as a backup to federal Marshals who will take into custody all of the crooks and "fun-and-games people" on Wall Street, and so forth. There is going to be a tremendous house-cleaning.

The reorganizational portions of the government itself should be concluded about 120 days after "disclosure". This 120 day period will begin with a formal announcement from the press-room of the **White House.**

This will give every reporter a clean shot at broadcasting the transition.

So these measures — *in terms of what the military wants* — they want to be the good guys. They're tired of being the bad guys. They would much rather be invited into a foreign country as a friend, and an assistant.

"You need some help? What do you need? Manpower? Bull-dozers? Food? We can come in and help you out."

"Yes! we're the United States Military! but we're the *new* one. We're the good guys." **BINGO!**

We think this new approach will work quite well.

We are not putting together any interim government. We are not trying to overthrow anything. We are trying to revert back to law and order, and create the smallest amount of chaos, *in the most peaceful fashion that we can*.

Our military cannot do this on their own for the simple reason that under the current structure, Obama is considered to be the President — *we all know that he is not* — he is the CEO (Chief Executive Officer) of a Corporation called THE UNITED STATES.

The majority of the American people do not understand this.

So as long as the American people recognize a criminal corporation in Washington D.C. as having jurisdiction over them — *and they do not stand up and say otherwise* — our military's hands are somewhat tied. They have been taking orders from a fake Commander in Chief.

As far as the financial people are concerned, they will never bring forth the money that's been intended for this country, these many years, until Washington is cleaned out, because if they did, the money would disappear down the black hole of theft, almost

immediately.

If the military are to once again take their orders from we the people, we have to be ready with a list of what we require it to do.

As pointed out above, this is temporary, and what gives the people the power and the authority and the standing to do this is simply **that a majority of states filed the same paperwork that Pennsylvania filed, putting the world on Notice that we have gone back under our *de jur* Constitution.**

We have reclaimed the Articles of Confederation, which have never been rescinded.

The Declaration of Independence and the Articles of Confederation are the basis of our freedom.

These arrests will mean the removal of the final obstacles that will allow for the implementation of the *new abundance systems* that are ready to free humanity from the current economy and its falsely imposed conditions of poverty and debt.

There are many men and women dedicated to this cause who have been working diligently in secret for years to bring us to this moment, who are eager to present to humanity the new system that will redistribute abundance to all,

and release humanity from the mundane life it has known.

Freedom is being returned to the people.

The release of withheld technologies and other suppressed elements will follow to assist this transition.

The news of these mass arrests will come sudden and come hard, and many who are unprepared with an understanding as to why, may feel shocked and confused to see so many ruling people taken into custody.

These people, how ever, have served to perpetuate our enslavement, and all have actively taken part in serious crimes against the people.

Certain big media groups have agreed to cover these events and assist in the **disclosure timeline.**

These arrests will be televised and fully shared with you, for it is owed to the people of the world that they witness the very moments and actions taken that will mean our release from the control of these people who have for so long worked to exploit and control humanity.

The manipulation will end and all humanity will enter into a new life. True freedom is to be returned to you!

Back Issues of the Maine Republic Email Alert:
http://www.scribd.com/maine_patriot_press

"ad Christi potentium et gloriam"
(for the power and glory of Christ)

Complaint and Motion for Summary Judgement or Jury Trial

Maine Republic Email Alert

No.241

". . . that I should bear witness unto the truth." — John 18:33 // David E. Robinson, Publisher

". . . if the trumpet give an uncertain sound, who shall prepare himself for battle?" — I Corinthians 14:8 —   09/15/12

Keshe Foundation call for and ultimatum for peace !

We have been asked to make our point clear about the upcoming expected and possible war between Israel, The United States, and Iran.

This new information below is being released to pre-empt any plans for a New War in the world.

We explain in this report how nations like Iran are made to appear as an Axis of evil in the eyes of the international community by pre-planned actions of some individual nations to start new international crises.

This a long read, but it is vital to understand why we speak to the nations of the earth at this time.

We are fully aware of what we are releasing so we want not only the nations but the citizens of the earth to understand the real depth of the Foundation's knowledge of the hidden agenda of the nations and the reasons for our actions; though sometimes they look as if they are against our true intentions.

The second part of this report will be soon released by the Foundation.

For those who do not know, we lay herein the basis of the Foundation's agenda for world peace.

It is our firm belief is that:

No war between Iran, Israel and the US shall occur, as the latter have more to lose, maybe everything, if such an action were to take place, and this is the clear message of the Foundation at this time. If you are interested in knowing why, take note of the following information in this open letter report.

It is easy to understand how a nation becomes an axis of evil according to the pre-mandated actions of the real evildoers of the earth.

Most of the individuals who have listened to my interviews, over the past years, know my educational background

and my work.

It is important for readers and the world to know that every nation can become part of an axis of evil according to the agreement signed by President Reagan and Mrs Thatcher in the late seventies for the establishment of a Nuclear Triad between The United States, The United Kingdom, and France.

There will be no war between Iran, Israel, The United States, and Iran as The United States has more and may be everything to lose if such an action werer to take place, and this is the clear message from this Foundation.

In my early work at the British nuclear classified site, I had an opportunity to read the proposal and documents which made it clear to me that the future of the nuclear industry of the world was well set, and per the agreement of the above three nations, the act of making every nation an axis of evil was signed and sealed by the leaders of these countries for the control of power and energy resources of the future.

In this agreement a process was initiated to bring the world economy to its knees and start a second process of slavery of all nations; as was done in earlier centuries with opium, but this time using the nuclear industry as a whip of threat and control.

In late seventies it was agreed that the British would use the military might of the United States to attack nations and rob them of their resources and control them by contolling their nuclear power supplies started by the British.

To make the triad work, the British gave the manufacturing rights of the nuclear power stations even for the UK to the US and their companies, with the carrot that the UK even stop all new research in development and building new nuclear British designed power stations, and the UK started the closure of all the nuclear power station capabilities of its own design.

In return the British, under the disguise of helping the US, accepted the recycling and proliferation of all nuclear fuel worldwide. This is the most lucrative part of the nuclear industry long term.

At the same time of this proliferation, in the future the UK can force nations to its will because if materials are not processed by the UK they cannot operate their nuclear power stations.

As nations need new fuel rods, their energy supply becomes slave to UK generosity and colonial power pressures as in the past.

This process has already started as the UK has been practising its reprocessing system by profiteering from fuel for Japan and Germany.

At the same time to keep the French on board, part of the structural work in Europe, and the nuclear fuel production of Europe, were given to the French.

Thus in this **triad of nations,** they have divided the future of the world energy supply between each other in such a way that once the oil runs out, or they create an oil crisis, these three nations — excluding Russia and China — will become the controllers of the energy for Europe, the Middle East, Asia and South

America.

Now let us explain how nations become an axis of evil in the eyes of the world like the nation of Iran through this *triad of nuclear control* through deliberate and false accusation and by controlling present world media.

• **First of all: Iran has been and is self-sufficient in producing raw nuclear material.**

In the mid-fifties the US used to take uranium from the mines of Hamadan in the south central regions of Iran for their nuclear processing and fuel supply, and this is well documented in international shipments of uranium.

Now these mines are in the hands of the Iranian nation, thus Iran does not need to purchase any fuel and is using its own natural resources for its future fuel processing and fuel production, and Iran even has surpluses of raw material to support other power stations of other nations if it is needed in the region for their future power supply.

Thus Iran has and can become a fuel supplier and competitor to the French and the US pieces of the pie of the present organised nuclear triad cabal.

• **Secondly: Iranian nuclear scientists with the help of the US in the past, and presently through work with Russian scientists, have gained enough knowledge to build nuclear reactors for power generation.**

Thus with the newly gained knowledge by home-grown and taught nuclear engineers and scientists, Iran now can and has cut into the piece of the pie of the US power generation manufacturing market.

So Iran becomes a financial threat to a member of nuclear triad, the USA.

By the same measure, Iranian aircraft engineers, being boycotted for parts by US sanctions, have made a full working Boeing 747 jetliner in Iran in the past five years to service the fleet of Iran jet liners so now one can buy exact parts of these craft in even better quality from Iran than from the US.

From producing these systems Iran is now using the same knowledge in building aircraft and has gained the full capability to produce spacecraft for the spaceship program of the present trials, using Iranian scientists.

Thus the US boycott has given Iran the advantage and lead for new spaceship and program systems that leave the space technology of NASA in the dark.

• **Thirdly, now that Iran has its own raw material and has learned the lessons of the oil refinery materials boycott by the west in the past thirty years, in the past three years Iran has begun the process of learning and developing the reprocessing of fuel.**

With this Iran can use its own mined uranium as fuel to enrich and use the fuel for supporting its nation with energy once the oil runs out.

Thus Iran with the capability of reprocessing and enriching fuel for its power stations now has the power and the knowledge to cut into the piece of cake of the UK of the triad.

Therefore now Iran has become a supplier and competitor not only in oil, but in the nuclear industry with the triad as well.

Thus the mask of the axis of evil is nothing but cover for the crimes of the past done by nations of the nuclear triad, so a new setting for the fuel crisis of 1972 exists, where this time the British will control world energy and will take nations hostage like pirates of the high seas as they have done for centuries in the past, but in a modern version.

The other recent action of the EU boycott against the nation of Iran came about purely by an accident and the greed of Germany which had nothing to do with Iran.

In the early seventies Iran acquired a small prototype nuclear reactor built for Iran by the western nations for training its future nuclear scientists for the power stations to be built in late and early eighties by them for Iran.

I was presumed to be one of these scientists when and if I returned to Tehran after finishing my education as a nuclear engineer in Europe.

This nuclear reactor in Tehran University has the capability of producing the low level high grade nuclear material isotopes needed nowadays in the medical sector of the health system of all nations.

This sector of the health radiation industry will be worth some 12 billion euros in the coming years.

What has happened in the past years is that the nuclear power plant which is the parallel system to the Iranian research nuclear reactor and has been the major producer of these isotopes for years, which was based in Canada and employing thousands of scientists and workers and generating billions of dollars of revenue for Canada for years, has gone faulty and cannot produce and supply the world demand for isotopes for the medical market.

Hence this has given a unprecedented chance to Iran to fill this vacuum generated in the market by chance in the western world supply of nuclear medical isotopes and this is a material to save lives of thousands of people around the world as without these isotopes no brain scan, no MRIs and other non-intrusive medical procedures can be carried out.

I wonder how many British, American, French and other nationals are NOT told daily that thanks to Iran we can give yours and your children's lives back to you.

This does not fit into the image of an axis of evil which the triad have made for Iran. I wonder how many Americans walk away from MRI tables and thank the lives of Iranian scientists who have filled the gap that was created by the Canada nuclear breakdown to save their lives.

We thank you Iranian nuclear scientists in the place of those who have never been told the real truth and salute you for your support of world citizens, even though in helping us you have put your lives in danger and are even losing your lives by assassination because you are serving and helping the rest of

Maine Republic *Email Alert* No.240

". . . that I should bear witness unto the truth." — *John 18:33* // *David E. Robinson, Publisher*

". . . if the trumpet give an uncertain sound, who shall prepare himself for battle?" — *I Corinthians 14:8* — 09/14/12

The Greatest "Disclosure" Ever to be Released to the World — by the Keshe Foundation

On 21 September 2012 the Keshe Foundation will release the first phase of its space technology and the gravitational and magnetic (Magravs) systems it has developed, to all scientists around the world simultaneously, for production and duplication.

From that point on, international borders will cease to have any real significance.

This is because, once the first flight system has been built and put into operation for the public, the time of travel for example from Tehran to New York will be about 10 minutes maximum.

The new airborne systems will enable every individual to make the same length of journey in the same time and at hardly any cost from any point on this planet.

The craft will not be detectable with present radar technology.

The energy crisis will be resolved at a stroke, and once the technology is put into practice the powers that control energy supplies and through them the present financial structures will find their hands empty.

The world water shortage will be addressed and resolved by presenting this technology to the public soon after the release of our energy and space technology.

How we have done this?

For the past six years we have used the international patent system to make sure that **every nation and major scientists around the world have a copy of our patents in their possession.**

(Please check the European patent and international servers downloads for identification number of downloads.)

Thus we have prevented any possible blocking of this technology by any individual or group and now most nations

Kf

Mehran Keshe
Nuclear Engineer
Plasma Technology
Generating Affordable, Renewable and Clean Energy for Electricity and Transportation

are in possession of our patents for energy generation, medical systems and space travel.

In this way the methods used in the past to prevent international development have been circumvented and now all nations have the same opportunity to work together to see that this technology is developed safely.

The principal point is that our technology is intended to be freely available to every government for the benefit of all its citizens.

Through the systems we have developed every nation can have access to as much energy, water and food as

they need, as well as to new methods of health care and of transport, all at very little cost.

According to its charter the Keshe Foundation and all its technologies are owned by the peoples of the world.

The patents are the assets of every individual on this planet and cannot be claimed by any one person or organization or nation.

This means that all income generated by the technology belongs to the nation that makes use of it.

The presentation on 21 September 2012 will be the first step in the Keshe Foundation's teaching program to share its knowledge and put it into the hands of the people worldwide.

Once these new technologies and their benefits are known to the general public, the leaders of every nation will need to decide how they are going to implement them for the betterment of everyone.

At that point there will be two choices:

1. Either we all work together to change the life of everybody on earth for the better through the correct patterns of conduct, or

2. The advanced nations of the world will see in the near future a flood of immigrants in tens of thousands flocking to the major cities.

We are prepared to present the technology to your representatives in any setting, so that they can understand its implications and the changes it will bring about.

From now on, we can make sure that no child or adult will die of thirst or hunger and that no nation will be attacked by another,

Because the potential military applications of the new technology are so horrendously destructive that we will have no choice but to accept that fighting over the resources of the planet is a thing of the past.

There has been nothing wrong with protecting national assets, but now, as the leaders of small regions of the Earth, it is Your responsibility to see that its resources are available to be shared, and that with the help of our technology, everyone's basic needs for energy, water, food and health care are met.

The Keshe Foundation takes no account of color, nationality, religion or political affiliation, thus our call is going out to every government to appoint a team of scientists to come and see our technologies at first hand.

Then they can decide whether or not to make use of them.

If you ignore this offer, your nation will soon have no choice but to follow the lead of the nations who have decided to develop them.

We call on your nation, to start the process of world cooperation as soon as possible because once these systems are in operation, the frontiers that separate one country from another will have no meaning.

We have set the scene for a change of course for humanity and in the coming months we will see it through.

In the near future people will come to realize that we are here to serve each other, and not to be served, as all resources will be available to everyone, at the same time, and in the same measure.

~ M T Keshe
The founder and caretaker director of Stichting the Keshe Foundation (The Netherlands).

To view an 'intro video': http://youtu.be/UrN99RELqwo

"ad Christi potentium et gloriam"
(for the power and glory of Christ)

Notice to the world - delivered to the Office of Private International Law at the Hague

We the people, the flesh and blood inhabitants, of the several nation states on the continent of North America, known as the united states of America, hereby declare and give **Notice** to the World herewith that;

We have assembled in our individual states and given **Notice** that by the authority of jural assembly in each state, having ratified a sovereign constitution for its own governance, declaring its own civil authority of independence, freedom and every power, jurisdiction and right which is not expressly delegated to the united states in honourable Congress assembled, by the will of the people.

We have assembled as a majority of the states with the purpose to return our Nation to its original design **according to the true belief and intention of the free people** under the Articles of Confederation, the original Constitution for the united states of America, the Declaration of Independence, the Northwest Ordinance, and the Bill of Rights, whereby we are a nation by the people, for the people and of the people.

These nation states assembled as a majority of the states hereby give **Notice** we **mandate our right of civil authority** to reclaim our freedom of governance from all usurpation of our Common Law structure so as to eliminate forevermore the existence of federal, state and local corporate entities in any position impersonating the original sovereign structure of government.

The nation states assembled as a majority of the states give **Notice** we intend to disavow any national affiliations with IMF, World Banks, United Nations, Federal Reserve and all other such organizations, as well as all alleged encumbrances and claims associated with the corporate United States, which were never created, sanctioned, or authorized according to the will of the people of the united states of America.

This assembly of the majority of nation states of the united states of America, including a quorum of the original thirteen states in Union, as empowered in Article 11 of the Articles of Confederation, do also hereby agree to the admission of, lay claim to, and empower all states not having completed documentation of Notice for inclusion in this **Notice** document, to be included nonetheless, either as nation states in Union, pending completion of documentation, or as developing Territories, unless specifically and individually declined by them.

"ad Christi potentium et gloriam"
(for the power and glory of Christ)

FedEx Express

February 7, 2012.

Dear Customer:

The following is the proof-of-delivery for tracking number
798019154282

Delivery Information:

Status:	Delivered
Signed for by:	L. MOLENA
Service type:	International Priority Service
Delivered to:	Receptionist/Front Desk
Delivery location:	SEE: RECIPIENT DETAILS
	THE HAGUE 2517
Delivery date:	Feb 7, 2012 14:45

Shipping Information:

Tracking Number:
798019154282
Ship Date:
Feb 3, 2012
Weight:
28.0 lbs/12.7 kg
Reference:
Nation/States project
Shipper:
M C MANAGEMENT SERVICES OF S FL
19411 NW CT
PEMBROKE PINES, FL 33029 US
Recipient:
PERMANENT BUREAU
HAGUE CONFERENCE ON PVT. INTL. LAW
SCHEVENINGSWEG 6
THE HAGUE 2517 NL

"ad Christi potentium et gloriam"

Complaint and Motion for Summary Judgement or Jury Trial

Was a US Spy Drone captured by an Iranian Flying Saucer?

Mehran Tavakoli Keshe, an Iranian nuclear scientist and engineer, claims that an Iranian flying saucer technology he developed was used to capture the Sentinel drone about which the mainstream media had been reportin last year. Does Iran have a space program more advanced than NASA's? Good Question!

Of all the inventors making bold claims on the internet, Iranian nuclear engineer Mehran Tavakoli Keshe is perhaps the most enigmatic, and the most interesting.

By allegedly harnessing a fusion reaction that manipulates dark matter, regular matter, and antimatter, he claims to have developed technologies that rival those in science fiction.

Keshe claims that years ago he gave the Iranian military his technology in order for them to produce flying saucers; and the alleged Iranian flying saucer that had popped up in the news last March was a result of that. He had offered it to NASA, but they poopooed it.

If his statements are true, these craft can do more than just manipulate gravity for propulsion. They can also produce force fields, emit tractor beams, generate unlimited amounts of clean energy, and have inertial damping systems that allow occupants to avoid feeling accelerations.

Keshe is now claiming in a post made to his forum that this technology was used by Iran to capture the unmanned Sentinel spy drone that the US military had sent over to spy ob Iran. He states that the drone was **snatched out of the air with force fields, then placed on**

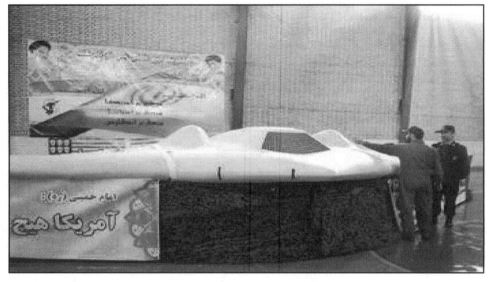

The US spy drone captured by the Iranians. Credit: <u>AFP</u>

the ground, without significant damage (as seen in the photo), **to be retrieved.**

This is very different than Iran's official story that claims the drone was captured with a "cyber attack" or hacking. If Keshe's claim is true, then the "official" story from Iran is a spin. According to the mainstream media, the method by which the drone was captured is "a mystery".

As he continues in his post, Keshe talks about how the Iranian saucer program is more advanced than NASA's space program. He describes it as being "light years" ahead of NASA. However, he makes it clear that the technology is not going to be used for aggressive purposes by the Iranian military, but only for peaceful purposes. He describes Iran as a peace-loving nation, which may not or just may be accurate.

In the same post, he invites the United States and other nations of the world to negotiate with the Keshe

Foundation for full disclosure and use of the technology. It seems that he is serious about wanting the technology to be used for the good of the planet, and not to give one nation's military an advantage over all others. Here is an excerpt.

There is no hacking but the use of advanced space technology.

In the past, in this forum, and in my presentations around Europe, and in my international interviews in the past months, I have explained again and again that the Keshe Foundation and Iranian spaceship program has the capability of radar blockage and capture of material in airborne condition.

The Islamic republic of Iran has the capability of **capturing and landing any flying object irrespective of their size and speed** *as seen with capture of* *one of the most advanced flying crafts in these above videos and the request of so called the most advanced nation on earth for its* toy back. In this case, there has been no malfunctioning of the craft, but this has been a simple capture and landing of an object at high speed through advanced space programs.

http://keshefoundation.com/phpbb/viewtopic.php?f=2&t=2209

What he may or may not realize, is that the black-budget, military-industrial-complex based in the United States has been testing advanced air and space craft for decades. Some of these very secret craft are probably using technology reverse-engineered from the extraterrestrial space craft that crashed near Roswell, NM in 1947.

After fifty or so years of working with ET technology, the military-industrial-complex more than likely has craft that rival those in Iran's nascent saucer program. The difference is that Keshe offers his technology to mankind, while the military-industrial-complex seques-ters their advanced technology for their own nefarious purposes. According to Keshe, Iran just happens to be the first to embrace his technology.

It is difficult to know if Keshe is telling the truth, if he is exaggerating, or if he is delusional. He has made so many extremely amazing claims, it is hard to believe all of them can be true. If they are "all" true, then he has developed every technology needed for humanity to colonize the galaxy.

Simply put, we would not need to wait hundreds of years to build the Starship Enterprise, we could build it right now!

For a review of his technology, see our feature page:

http://peswiki.com/index.php/Directory:Keshe_Foundation

Keshe seems to be starting to provide some limited amount of evidence to back up his assertions. He claims that there was a demonstration during a one and a half hour lecture in Belgium on December 3, 2011, organized by the Belford Group of Belgium.

According to Keshe, 130 people attended the demonstration. During the event, he asserts a video recording of a laboratory system was shown, that had weight reducing abilities. Afterwards, the actual weight reducing system was demonstrated to the audience. In addition, a 3-4 kilowatt generator was presented, along with an "Oasis" system.

An article found on the wanttoknow.nl website discusses a lecture he gave in the Netherlands, in November of this year. The author of the article describes how during the lecture he showed a video of a three kilowatt generator, but then claimed he could not demonstrate it there, because the police had stolen it from him.

Repeatedly, Keshe claims to be the victim of suppression by various governments and organizations. For example, in Toronto he had all of his papers stolen by Canadian government officials. If his technology works as he claims, I think suppression of his technology is very likely, because it could change the world if widely adopted.

If Keshe's claims have any veracity, this is one of the most amazing developments taking place on the planet.

"ad Christi potentium et gloriam"
(for the power and glory of Christ)

Maine Republic Email Alert

No.244

". . . that I should bear witness unto the truth." — John 18:33 // David E. Robinson, Publisher

". . . if the trumpet give an uncertain sound, who shall prepare himself for battle?" — I Corinthians 14:8 — 09/18/12

Part II - Was a US Spy Drone captured by an Iranian Flying Saucer?

Part II - Mehran Keshe of the Keshe Foundation claims that the advanced space technology he gave the Iranian military a few years ago, was used to capture the Sentinel spy drone.

Keshe claims saucer craft were able to pick the drone out of the sky with force fields, and bring it down from its 20,000 foot cruising altitude to the ground in tact.

We reviewed his claims in part one (Issues #242), titled, "Was a US Spy Drone Captured by an Iranian Flying Saucer."

Now, Sterling Allan, the founder of PESN, has conducted an hour and a half long interview with Keshe. The interview spans a wide array of topics, covering everything from Iranian saucer technology, free energy technology, and even global politics.

As the interview began, Keshe reiterated his claim that the Iranian military used advanced space technology (far beyond anything NASA may have) to capture the Sentinel spy drone. He claims the proof of this is that the drone was barely damaged in the photos released by the Iranian military. According to him, if the drone had been shot down or simply hacked into, it would have crashed and been destroyed.

The guidance technology on that drone is the most sophisticated navigation technology on the planet, at least among the non-black-budget projects. Interception required jamming the guidance signal that would trigger it to self-destruct in the case of hacking or other interference.

Allegedly, the technology used by the Iranian military to build their saucer fleet was given to them by the Keshe Foundation. The technology does not only offer an advanced means of

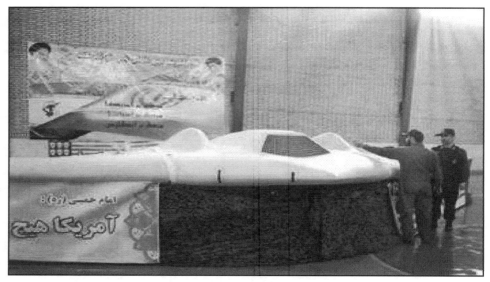

The US spy drone captured by the Iranians.Credit: <u>AFP</u>

propulsion, but also inertial damping, tractor beams, force fields, and the ability to jam radar. He states that although the Iranian military was the first to acquire the technology, he has also given the technology to the Belgian government, along with another undisclosed nation. He claims that Canada stole some of his technology when they seized all his papers and materials when he was on a trip through Toronto.

When it comes to the potential use of the technology for warfare, Keshe stated that he wants all nations to acquire the technology. He claims if all nations have the technology, then no nation will have an advantage over others who do not; and its primary advantage is defensive, not offensive.

A variation of the same technology that is said to allow for advanced propulsion is also asserted to allow for the clean production of electricity. Keshe is taking deposits for both 3-4 kilowatt power generators that require a 500 Euro

deposit, and 10 kilowatt power generators that require a 2,000 Euro deposit. The full price of the 3-4 kilowatt system is five thousand Euro, and the full price of the 10 kilowatt system is twenty thousand Euro. However, he stated the prices for both systems are about to go up, due to high demand. During the interview he explained how these systems are far more economical and advantageous than solar powered systems. They run twenty four hours a day, unlike solar panels that only operate in the day time, and they are cheaper than solar power systems. They also are claimed to only require refueling once every thirty to fifty years. These systems are also sealed to prevent anyone from opening them up and seeing how they work.

Keshe claims they started manufacturing the first ten thousand units six months ago. The first units should start shipping to customers in about six months. He mentioned that if the units are not shipped within 12 months the deposits will be returned. He described how the deposits are sitting in a secure bank account, completely untouched. A story was told about how once someone complained about how the deposits were being managed. Keshe said that two governments examined the bank account the deposits were held in, and determined everything was in order.

In the near future, after the ten thousand units are delivered, the profits generated will be used to open a university where students will learn about the technology. They had approached established universities requesting access to their facilities, but their requests were denied.

A long conversation began about the concept of free energy, and the implications in regards to government revenue. Keshe made it clear that he did not want to disrupt the status-quo, and was cooperating with governments to make sure they would be able to tax the energy produced by his systems, or the systems themselves. It seems he thinks taxes on fuel and energy are the main source of revenue for many nations, and there are no alternatives. Sterling Allan brought up the idea of reducing the size of government so such taxes would not be needed. Keshe still insisted taxes would be needed.

Repeatedly, he stated that people have the wrong idea about free energy, because they will not be able to use it without paying taxes on it. If people did not pay taxes on free energy, kids would not be educated, the old would not be looked after, infrastructure would deteriorate, etc... My opinion is that free energy technology will stimulate the economy so much that no such taxes will be needed, because the tax revenue from other sources will increase. For example, if more people get jobs due to new factories being built to manufacture millions of free energy devices, then they will actually be earning money so they will have to pay more to the income tax. In addition, they will be buying more goods so they will be paying more sales tax. They will be paying other taxes as well. Right now, one reason why so many nations are bankrupt is because their people are bankrupt. When people are

broke and out of work, they are not paying taxes. If free energy technology can put people to work, then governments will be able to generate revenue without creating any new taxes.

According to Keshe, he has been given one or two lectures a week for many months. Most of these lectures have been held in Europe. He claims to have demonstrated multiple technologies in a recent lecture in Belgium, but he required that everyone put their cameras and cell phones in black bags, to prevent any pictures from being taken. In 2012 there will be many more such lectures. The lectures will also have different topics. Some of them will be about the energy producing aspects of the technology, others will be about the medical applications, and others will be about the space travel aspect of the technology. Many of these lectures will be held at the Keshe Foundation facilities that have a room that can host 130 people.

Keshe sees his technology as benefiting space travel more than anything else. It allegedly solves all the problems relating to space flight.

Here is a short list of what it is capable of accomplishing, according to him.

· **Extremely fast speeds** that would allow for rapid travel through the solar system and beyond. A round trip to Mars, with a stop at the moon, would take a few days.

· **Deflector fields** that can destroy tiny particles that could impact and destroy a vehicle traveling at high speed.

· **Friction removal**, so there is no effect from environmental friction as the vehicle travels through the atmosphere.

· **Inertial damping** so that the occupants of a craft would not feel accelerations.

· **Force fields** that can block space radiation.

· **Artificial gravity** so that the occupants would be able to live and work just like they do on Earth, without having to worry about the effect of weightlessness on their body.

· **Invisibility** or cloaking technology.

· Replicators or the ability to turn

energy into **food** and **water**.

· **Healing** technology to address injuries or sickness that might arise.

Over the last year he has also gained new supporters, and describes the Keshe Foundation as being "cash rich." He claims they do not need partners to help manufacture products. They have the money and facilities they need. If a serious company wants to distribute products, they can come to them and put in an order. When the products are ready they will be notified, and they can pick them up.

When Sterling asked who should a potential interested party contact to get confirmation the technology works, Keshe stated that they show everything to serious parties. If a company is interested in the technology, they should go directly to the foundation. They would provide them with the information they need. However, they ignore the "lunatics" that are not serious, and do not really want to help them.

Other technologies the Keshe Foundation is working on were also talked about. They have medical technologies that are claimed to allow paralyzed individuals to re-gain their ability to walk. Some time ago they offered to use the technology to help congresswoman Giffords, who was shot in the head. Also, they claim to have a technology that can create water and food anywhere — on Earth or in space. For space travel, it is claimed the technology transforms the gaseous carbon that is emitted from breathing into solid carbon, that can "have some things added to it", and can be consumed as food. This product is claimed to be in human trials.

Keshe announced during the interview that a deal had been made to commercialize devices using his technology that somehow produces water by extracting it from the humidity in the air. Instead of using condensation methods, the technology uses magnetic fields. The resulting water is said to be completely pure. This would be potentially a better solution than obtaining water from condensation systems, because pollution from the atmosphere can contaminate the water they produce. Keshe's method allegedly attracts only

Complaint and Motion for Summary Judgement or Jury Trial

the water molecules from the surrounding, and nothing else.

The subject of Iran's image around the world was also discussed. Keshe repeatedly claimed that Iran is a peaceful nation. He claims that Iran will never use the saucer technology to attack other nations. However, he did say that if the United States or another nation sent a missile to hit Iran, that they have the technology to send it back at whoever sent it, or to deflect it out to space, because nuclear explosions anywhere on earth impact the entire planet, as illustrated by the Chernoble and Fukushima disasters.

During the call he also thanked Iran and Belgium for supporting his research.

When the topic of UFOs was brought up, Keshe made it clear he does not think extraterrestrials are visiting our planet. He thinks that there is life elsewhere in the universe, but ETs are not flying in our skies. Despite the fact that nations like the United States have black budget programs working on advanced, top secret aircraft, he does not think that there is any space technology in the world that can compete with his.

It is difficult to determine the truth about these claims. I see three possibilities.

Keshe is the most important scientist in the history of mankind, and is about to push humanity into an amazing new era of almost "too good to be true" technology.

Keshe has a theory and is working on a product, but is exaggerating about what has been accomplished with the technology.

Keshe is delusional and needs mental help.

I think that all three have an equal probability of being true.

Regardless if he is a hero or an insane madman, his story is interesting. I'm really hoping he is telling the truth, and his claims are accurate. If they are, the future is about to become very exciting!

Source:
Part I - http://tinyurl.com/8bbtof3
Part II - http://tinyurl.com/9hhfzh8

Iran Video of captured US Drone
http://tinyurl.com/culpx5j
2 hr. Interview with M.T. Keshe
http://tinyurl.com/8q9c2cx
2-1/2 hr. Interview with M.T. Keshe
http://tinyurl.com/9ezh66v

"ad Christi potentium et gloriam"
(for the power and glory of Christ)

GOVERNMENT WITHOUT THE INCOME TAX

One of the major limitations on the Government power, the "power of the purse", was susbverted in 1913.

When the "Federal Reserve System" and the "Federal income tax" were created in 1913,they destroyed all reasonable limitations on how much money the Federal Government had access to.

They also destroyed all reasonable limitations on the Federal Government's ability to expand far beyond its constitutional role.

When discussing the issue of taxation, the average American has a tendency to defend the "income tax" as being necessary to fund government at the Federal level.

The Assertion:

As for the income tax, only an anarchist thinks a country can survive without taxation.

My Rebuttal:

These are two separate issues,

One: - needing "taxes" to finance government,

Two: - whether of not an INCOME tax is needed to finance our FEDERAL GOVERNMENT.

This country did not have a *federal income tax* prior to 1913.

America went from "start up" in 1776 to the most prosperous nation on the planet without an "income tax" let alone the intrusive, bloated, and "unconstitutional" government that goes with it.

Corporate taxes, taxes on alcohol, tobacco, firearms, tariffs on trade, military hardwares sales, etc., would be more than enough to fund the "constitutionally limited" federal Government established by our founding fathers.

If the income tax were abolished today, the Federal government would still have more than a TRILLION dollars annually to fund its operations, even after *adjusting for inflation*, an obscene amount of money compared to what it used to operate on.

A huge percentage of the income taxes collected today do nothing to fund government programs.

The money is simply burned away as interest payments on the debt that our "leaders" have accumulated for us to pay.

The actual cost of all those programs increases drastically when you include the added expense of interest payments.

Currently, interest payments on our 16 Trillion dollar debt are costing American taxpayers about $80 Million dollars PER HOUR; approximately $720 Billion a year!

Now, you'd think our elected officials would be a little worried about this; all that money being wasted on interest payments.

More specifically, they are currently adding more than $90 Million dollars PER HOUR to the debt we already have.

The "income tax" is just part of the equation.

The other part, also created in 1913, is the Federal Reserve Banking System; supposedly created to act as an exclusive lender to our ambitious friends in Washington, DC.

Now, instead of having to go to the American people for money, the government can just go to their good friends at the Federal Reserve.

"The Fed" Bankers are happy to *loan* whatever is requested.

Consider this:

When you and I "give money" to the government, it COSTS us money.

When the bankers "give money" to the government the bankers EARN money, for themselves.

So, the bigger the government gets and the more debt it acquires, on our tab, the greater the benefit to the bankers.

This system is antithetical (destructive) to the concept of "limited government."

Their final aim is nothing less than the destruction of our American sovereignty! and the merger of all nations into a financially controlled "one world" government!

Can we support our Federal Government without an income tax? That depends.

The corrupt, overgrown, unconstitutional government we currently have? Absolutely not.

The constitutionally limited government America was supposed to have? Absolutely!

If we don't gain control of this "creature" that is feeding on our country, we sill facilitate the destruction of everything America was meant to be.

Rest assured that won't happen be accident; it will come to us *by design.*

We are being led into slavery, and to slaughter, by a group of pathological liars who, ironically, are being *well payed,* to protect us.

Something for Nothing

The Federal Reserve System was created in secrecy by a handful of powerful bankers.

The first step was to create money out of nothing.

Now we know that the bankers "loan out" money that they do not possess.

Let's say you need to borrow $200,000.

The bankers simply key-stroke in "$200,000" into your checking account, and poof, they just created $200,000 dollars!

As soon as this $200,000 is loaned to you, and you sign on the dotted line, it is entered into the bank's books as an asset.

You signed a contract that says you owe the bank $200,000, plus interest, and it is assumed that you will pay in back.

However, your loan is also entered into the bank's books, as a liability.

It is assumed that you will go out and spend the $200,00 dollars worth of checkbook money that *you recently created* and your bank will be *liable* for those checks.

Many of the checks that you write will end up in other banks, and that means that the issuing bank, your bank, will owe potentially up to $200,000 as those _cashed_ checks start rolling in.

Being able to earn interest on money created out of thin air is a sweet deal for the bank.

If it takes 30 years to repay your loan, the bank will _earn for itself_ hundreds of thousands of dollars in interest on the money it _loaned_ to you.

SAMPLE FREEDOM OF INFORMATION ACT REQUEST

Dear Disclosure Officer:

This is a request under the FREEDOM OF INFORMATION ACT at 5 USC 552 and PRIVACY ACT at 5 USC 552(a). This request does not fall under exception 26 USC § 6103(e)(7). These documents are not sought for any commercial purposes. This is my firm promise to pay fees and costs for locating and duplicating the records requested below..

Understanding exemptions are discretionary, rather than mandatory, if for some reason you determined any portion of this request to be exempt from release, please furnish the following (a) those portions reasonably segregateable after the exempt material is deleted, (b) detailed justification for your discretionary exemption since the overriding objective of the FOIA is to maximize public access to agency records, and (c) provide the name of the official and correct address to whom an administrative appeals should be addressed.

I am attesting under the penalty of perjury under the laws of the united States of America 28 U.S.C. § 1746(1), that I am a category 5 CFR 294.103(d) requester.

Please provide copies of the documents responsive to my request, or state there are no documents responsive to my request. I make this request for copies of documents, in lieu of personal inspection of same

Please provide **the OMB control Number & an actual copy of the properly registered and OMB approved form <u>for government collection of information from people living within the 50 states</u>** relating to 26 U.S.C. § 1040 titled "**<u>Transfer of certain farm, etc., real property</u>**".

Should you decide this request has been sent to the wrong office, please make certain that you forward this to the proper office and notify me of same.

I understand the penalties provided in 5 USC 552 (a)(i)(3) for requesting or obtaining access to records under false pretenses.

Respectfully submitted,

Requester, All rights reserved.

Enclosure: Photocopy of Drivers License enclosed to provide proof of Identification.

David E. Robinson
3 Linnell Circle
Brunswick, Maine 04011

July 23, 2012

United States Senator Susan M. Collins
One Canal Plaza, Suite 802
Portland, Maine 04101

Re: Oaths of Office to support and defend the Constitution for the United States of America (1781-1791)

Dear Senator Collins,

I believe that no public official should be admonished or disciplined for wrongdoing until the requirements of the Golden Rule have been strictly obeyed.

As you know the Constitution for the United States of America is being grossly ignored by government officials today even though *all public officials* "shall be bound by oath or affirmation to support this Constitution..." (Art. 6 cl. 3).

Because of the high regard which your constituents and I hold for you, I am writing to ask you to help us resolved the conflicting situation we now face.

I have taken preparatory steps to file a Citizen Complaint against you with the Cumberland County Sheriff in Portland, Maine, based on the website report at http://tinyurl.com/c4pctsj that lists you — and many other government officials — as having committed a Violation Worthy of Arrest.

All Americans need to be awakened to the vital importance of obeying the Constitution of the United States of America as our Founding Fathers presented it to us to hopefully save us from any Treasonous Acts of our government; especially today in the wake of the Red Flag, Movie Theater Massacre in Colorado prior to the upcoming vote on the United Nation's Small Arms Treaty that must not pass.

The Second Amendment to our Constitution is currently, as you know, under threat.

Please allow me to file this complaint with your blessings?

I await your reply to this honorable request.

Sincerely,
Your constituent,

David Everett Robinson
http://maine-patriot.com

NOTICE OF REQUEST FOR CLARIFICATION

I acknowledge and accept your oath of office.

Due to the inability to comprehend and therefore inability to understand the IRS code, I took it upon myself to study and it seems no matter what I do, I get indications that I have done something wrong and you penalize or attempt to penalize me for it.

More information has surfaced and I can see why you get confused why I send anything in.

As I have become aware of a few facts, I wonder if you or someone can answer them.

I want to provide you with all of the information that the law demands or requires. In order to do so I must first comprehend the facts involved. I do not understand the tax laws, rules, or regulations. I do not wish to do anything wrong, nor do I want to be mislead.

1. Do I have Unalienable Rights?

2. Do I have a right to contract with whom I choose?

3. Do I have a Right to earn a living?

4. Can a right be taxed?

5. Is it true that Federal Reserve Notes are debt obligations to the US government? (*Title 18 § 8*)

6. Is it true that debt obligations of the United States are non taxable and exempt from taxation? (*Title 31 § 3124*)

7. Is it true that you cannot tax an estate? (*Title 31 § 3124*)

8. Is it true that Federal Reserve Notes are securities? (*Title 12 § 411*)

9. Is it true that the courts have ruled that Federal Reserve notes are worthless pieces of paper that are void? (*14th Amendment § 4*)

10. Is it True that Giving Federal Reserve notes does not constitute payment? (*Echart v. Commissioners C.C.C 42 Fd2d 158*)

11. Is it true that notes are not good and lawful money of the United States? (*Rains v State, 226 S.W. 189*).

12. Is it true that a 'note' is only a promise to pay? (*Fidelity Savings v Grimes, 131 P2d 894*)

13. Is it true that there is no gold or silver backing these Federal Reserve notes? (*News; Federal Reserve Board, Congress, President, Courts, IRS*)

14. Is it true that Federal Reserve notes are worthless securities? (*Title 26 § 165 (g)(2)(C)*)

15. Is it true that according to the Constitution that payment of debts must be in gold or silver? (*Article 1 §10, Article 1 § 8 ¶, Law of Nations Book 1 Chapter X § 105-107*)

16. Is it true that there is no Amendment that abrogates the requirement for money to be in gold or silver?

17. Is it true that the government is to settle claims? (*Title 31 § 3702*)

18. Is it a fact that gov't Agencies must respond to the arguments made to them? (*Lwin V. I.N.S., 144 F3d 505*)

19. It is true that all agents of the government have sworn an oath to protect, defend, and obey the constitution?

20. Is it true that willful disobedience of the oath of office is an act of <u>treason</u>?

21. Is it true that you must obey court decisions?

22. Is this true that "there is a clear distinction between 'profit' and 'wages', or a compensation for labor. Compensation for labor (wages) cannot be regarded as profit within the meaning of the law.

The word 'profit', as ordinarily used, means the gain made upon any business or investment — a different thing altogether from the mere compensation for labor." (*Oliver v. Halstead, 86 S.E. Rep 2nd 85e9 (1955)*).

23. Is it true that "**the claim that salaries, wages, and compensation for personal services are to be taxed as an entirety,** and therefore must be returned by the individual who has performed the services which produce the gain, **is without support**... and that **salaries, wages, or compensation for personal services are not ... gains, profits, and income derived from salaries, wages, or compensation for personal services.**" (*Lucas v. Earl, 281 U.S. 111 (1930)*).

24. Is this true? "...**income must have the essential feature of <u>gain</u> to the recipient.** This was true when the 16th Amendment became effective, it was true at the time of Eisner v. Macomber Supra, it was true under Section 22(a) of the Internal Revenue Code of 1938, and it is likewise true under Section 61(a) of the I.R.S. Code of 1954. **If there is no gain, there is no income ... Congress has taxed <u>income</u> not <u>compensation</u>.**" (*Conner v. U.S., 303 F Supp. 1187 (1969)*).

25. Is this true? "The phraseology of **form 1040 is obscure** .... But it matters little what it does mean; the statute and the statute alone determines what is income to be taxed. **It taxes only income "<u>derived</u>"** from many different sources; **one does not "<u>derive income</u>" by rendering services and charging for them... the IRS cannot enlarge the scope of the statute.**" (*Edwards (vs.) Keith, 231 F110, 113 (1916)*).

26. Is this true? "**reasonable compensation for labor or services rendered is not profit.**" (*Lauderdale Cemetary Assoc. v. Mathews, 345 PA 239; 47 A. 2d 277, 280 (1946)*)

27. Has this been overturned? "**The individual, unlike the corporation, cannot be taxed for the mere privilege of existing.** The corporation is an <u>artificial entity</u> which owes its existence and charter powers to the state; **but the individuals' Right to**

live and own property are natural rights for the enjoyment of which an excise cannot be imposed.**" (*Corn v. Fort, 95 S.W. 2d 620 (1936) 28*). **The individual,** unlike the corporation, **cannot be taxed for the mere privilege of existing.** (*Redfield et al. V. Fisher et al.: 135 Or. 180, 292 P. 813*).

The corporation is an artificial entity which owes its existence and charter powers to the state; but **the individuals many enumerated rights to live and own property are natural rights for the enjoyment of which an excise cannot be imposed. (*26 R. C. L. Taxation § 209, p. 236; Cooley Taxation (4th Ed.) § 1676; In re Opnn of the Justices, 195 Mass. 607, 84 N. E. 499,29*).**

Am I considered to be a corporation? How would I correct this misconception? What proof do you have that makes and supports this claim?

30. Does this apply to you, the IRS or its agents? **18 USC 2071 - Concealment, removal, or mutilation generally,**

(a) Whoever willfully and unlawfully conceals, removes, mutilates, obliterates, or destroys, or attempts to do so, or, with intent to do so, takes and carries away any record, proceeding, map, book, paper, document, or other thing, filed or deposited with any clerk or officer of any court of the United States, or in any public office, or with any judicial or public officer of the United States, **shall be fined** under this title or imprisoned not more than three years, or both.

(b) Whoever, having the custody of any such record, proceeding, map, book, document, paper, or other thing, willfully and unlawfully conceals, removes, mutilates, obliterates, falsifies, or destroys the same, **shall be fined** under this title or imprisoned not more than three years, or both; **and shall forfeit** his office and be disqualified from holding any office under the United States. As used in this subsection, the term "office" does not include the office held by any person as a retired officer of the Armed Forces of the United States.

31. Are you not bound by these conditions? **Title 26 § 7214, Offenses By Officers And Employees Of The United States,**

(a) Unlawful acts of revenue officers or agents: Any officer or employee of the United States acting in connection with any revenue law of the United States . . .

(1) **who is** guilty of any extortion or willful oppression under color of law; or

(2) who knowingly demands other or greater sums than are authorized by law, or receives any fee, compensation, or reward, except as by law prescribed, for the performance of any duty; or

(3) who with intent to defeat the application of any provision of this title fails to perform any of the duties of his office or employment; or

(4) who conspires or colludes with any other person to defraud the United States; or

(5) who knowingly makes opportunity for any person to defraud the United States; or

(6) who does or omits to do any act with intent to enable any other person to defraud the United States;

(7) or who makes or signs any fraudulent entry in any book, or makes or signs any fraudulent certificate, return, or statement; or

(8) who, having knowledge or information of the violation of any revenue law by any person, or of fraud committed by any person against the United States under any revenue law, fails to report, in writing, such knowledge or information to the Secretary; or

(9) who demands, or accepts, or attempts to collect, directly or indirectly as payment or gift, or otherwise, any sum of money or other thing of value for the compromise, adjustment, or settlement of any charge or complaint for any violation or alleged violation of law, except as expressly authorized by law so to do . . . **shall be dismissed from office or discharged from employment** and, upon conviction thereof, shall be fined not more than $10,000, or imprisoned not more than 5 years, or both.

The court may in its discretion **award out of the fine so imposed an amount,** not in excess of one-

half thereof, **for the use of the informer,** if any, who shall be ascertained by the judgment of the court.

The court also shall render judgment against the said officer or employee for the amount of damages sustained in favor of the party injured, to be collected by execution. (c) Cross reference:

For penalty on collecting or disbursing officers trading in public funds or debts of property, see 18 U.S.C. 1901.

32. Is it true that any action without answering these questions is an act depriving me of my rights? (***Title 18 § 242, or if more than one of you, Title 18 § 242, Title 42 § 1983***),

33. Is it true if you have no lawful authority to contact me or demand "pay" anything without justification, **that it may be <u>extortion</u>.** (*Title 18 § 872, 878*).

34. It is true that only "any <u>officer</u>, <u>employee</u>, or <u>elected official</u>, of the United States, the District of Columbia, or any agency or instrumentality of the United States or the District of Columbia," may be levied? (***26 USC § 6331***).

A.) If this is true, <u>when was I elected</u> or <u>how did I become an officer</u>, or <u>employee</u> of the United States, the District of Columbia, agency or an instrumentality of the United States or District of Columbia?

35. If it is true that Federal Reserve Notes can only be used in the government of the United States, as outlined below:

January 30, 1934. HR 6976: An Act to protect the currency system of the United States.

Sec. 15 - **As used in this Act the term "United States" means the Government of the United States**; The term "currency of the United States" means **currency** which is legal tender in the United States, and **includes** United States notes, Treasury notes of 1890, gold certificates, silver certificates, Federal Reserve notes, and **circulating notes** of Federal Reserve banks and national banking associations; if this is true please file charges **against** the banks due to <u>loaning me currency outside their jurisdiction</u> and <u>without notification of such a limitation</u>.

Upon having these questions answered **under penalty of perjury** of the United States, I will seek a proper response to your requests.

It is my goal to obey all applicable laws, rules, and regulations as conscience [My God, King and Savior] commands me to do.

I am an ambassador for the kingdom of heaven with full power of attorney to do all acts in the name of my King, including debts, sins and trespasses.

If you claim that this is frivolous, **I would say that these laws, rules, regulations are the very foundation of our free society, and that as a public servant, you have a duty to respond** so that I would do what is right, fair and within the parameters of the intent.

Would you have me believe we have disregarded the constitution completely and that the IRS is not a terrorists agency? I cannot accept that.

However, if you insist that these questions are frivolous then **I must also remind you, that the burden of proof is upon the IRS, specifically the Secretary of the Treasure of Puerto Rico, to prove that** any court decision that has decided that court decision, congress, the laws of this great nation is invalid because you say so without any proof.

I would need the following :
1. The name(s) of the person(s) imposing the penalty.
2. A copy(s) of the job description(s) of that person(s) to verify that he/she has the authority to impose the penalty.
3. A copy of the legislative regulation that implements IRC 6702 into law, (Not interpretive or procedural regulations).

I am not a protestor, tax protestor, insurrectionist, rebellious, nor terrorists, I am a living flesh and bloo**d man, i.e. non-fiction**, with a few questions that need to be responded to.

In fact, **I am not arguing with you at all.** In order to properly respond; **I just need a few facts answered,** as this is what you would want, a proper response.

If it turns out that I need to file some form or pay for some liability that exists, or doesn't exist, I will be happy to accept it for value and settle and close the accounting for that year.

With or without your statement under penalty of perjury, I will require a voucher or coupons for the amount you claim I owe, if any.

If no response statement is made under penalty of perjury, I must assume that no liability or requirement on my behalf is warranted, that this might be a cause of action of "unjust enrichment", and that for any information you require, my time is chargeable at $400 per hour.

Please let me know exactly what you want and I will set up a fee schedule and/or a payment plan for you to pay me.

My rates are based in Gold or Silver currency, for the United States Constitutional guarantees me Republican form of government demands, and knowing that no gold or silver based currencies exists in the democracy, I will be happy to settle for Federal Reserve Notes at the current exchange rate, this is to say, not dollar for dollar.

I will also accept currencies of other foreign governments at the exchange rate of their currency compared to Federal Reserve Notes and then exchanged at the gold and silver rate.

I accept for value your claims, forgive these debts and return them for value.

Please contact your administrator directly.

Looking forward to your timely response.
Sincerely,

THE BEST KEPT SECRETS OF THE IRS

Introduction

In order to legally and safely beat the IRS it is necessary for you to adopt a certain frame of mind. You need to have a certain independence of mind. You need to be able to read the U.S. Constitution for yourself. You need to be able to recognize how the Supreme Court "judges" and other politicians routinely violate the Constitution. You need to realize that practically all lawyers and accountants are handmaidens of the **"terrorcrats"** - terrorist bureaucrats or coercive government agents. If you cannot already think for yourself, you need to learn to do so. You need to be able to think and do what is contrary to the entrenched among your family and friends. You need to become the authority of your own life. These and related issues are covered in the many other reports.

The Best Kept Secrets of the IRS

• The Sixteenth Amendment, allegedly giving Congress the power to collect income taxes, was never ratified.

For the compelling evidence, read **The Law That Never Was,** available from Common Sense Press, PO Box 1544, Billings, MT 59103.

The 16th Amendment, even if it had been ratified, is just a smokescreen that doesn't grant any new taxing powers to Congress.

The Supreme Court found in 1916 in the case **Brushaber v. Union Pacific R.R. Co., 240 U.S. 1,** that the 16th Amendment **didn't extend the taxing powers of Congress.**

• The Constitution does not empower Congress to delegate any function to the IRS.

• The IRS is a private corporation registered in Delaware.

• The IRS is the Gestapo of the Federal Reserve bankers; the same sponsors pushed the Federal Reserve Act and the Sixteenth Amendment through Congress in 1913.

• The purpose of the IRS is not to collect taxes but to control and terrorize people.

• It is doubtful whether money collected by the IRS goes to the government. Checks received by the IRS appear to be deposited by the Federal Reserve bankers, with "FRB" (for "Federal Reserve Bank") stamped on returned checks.

• The IRS has no jurisdiction in the 50 states, according to the limitations placed by the Constitution on the federal government.

• The Internal Revenue Code is not law.

• The Internal Revenue Code defines the term "person" in such a way that it does not apply to most Americans.

• The income tax is voluntary for most Americans.

• The income tax is an indirect excise tax. The final recipient of income cannot be liable for the income tax.

• The term "income" is so defined in the tax code that wages or salaries do not constitute "income."

• Corporations may only withhold taxes from an employee's earnings if the employee specifically requests such withholding. No one can be legally forced to complete a W4 withholding form.

• Employers who withhold part of the salaries or wages of employees against the will of the employee, commit theft.

• The U.S. Constitution effectively defines "money" as gold and silver - Article I, Section 10:

"No State shall make anything but gold and silver coin a tender in payment of debts."

The law agrees: "The terms 'lawful money' and "lawful money of the United States' shall be construed to mean gold or silver coin of the United States." (**12**

USC 152).

The Federal Reserve Note is not money; it is counterfeit currency, hence receipts in Federal Reserve Notes, having no legal value, are not taxable.

• Most Americans can relinquish their "U.S. Citizenship" and declare themselves as State Citizens subject neither to Federal nor State income taxes.

• There is a legal principle **"void for vagueness"**. The tax code is in many parts so vague that nobody (**including IRS terrorcrats**) can understand it.

A 1991 Supreme Court case found that if someone sincerely believes that he or she doesn't have to file a tax return and pay income tax, then that person cannot be convicted of a crime; several other courts have found accordingly.

• In 1991, the Fifth Circuit Court of Appeals held that if someone claims they are not subject to the federal income tax, then the burden to prove to the contrary is on the IRS. For most Americans the IRS can't won't even attempt prove this via an Affidavit signed under the penalty of perjury.

• Filing a 1040 or other tax return involves the surrender of your Fifth Amendment right to not incriminate oneself. The Fifth Amendment of the Constitution says that no one can be forced to incriminate himself or herself.

• All IRS liens and seizures are illegal.

• The IRS in its totality is a violent, criminal, extortion racket with no legal basis whatsoever.

• There are methods for protecting income and assets so that no matter what the IRS terrorcrats do it becomes difficult for them to violate your unalienable rights to own property and the fruits of your labor. **One way is to use Trusts.**

• In his book *Tax Fraud & Evasion: The War Stories*, Attorney Donald W. MacPherson exposes the IRS as a **paper tiger**. The probability that any individual would be prosecuted for not paying taxes to the IRS are about 70,000 to one. The probability that any individual will go to jail for not paying taxes are about 150,000 to one.

A Call to Action

Practically everything the federal government does is evil, unconstitutional, criminal, and highly destructive. The IRS Gestapo plays a major role in keeping the criminal terrocrats in power. The IRS needs to be eliminated. In the words of Attorney Donald W. MacPherson, "The Beast must be destroyed." What federal government we need (if any) can be financed through voluntary exchange for valuable products and services produced, augmented by voluntary contributions.

QUESTIONS AND ANSWERS

1. Is it possible for Americans to legally stop paying income taxes?

It is possible for most Americans to legally stop paying both federal and state income taxes. This applies to most Americans who live and work in the 50 States. It does not necessarily apply to Americans working for the federal government, or those who work in federal military installations. The central issue here is federal jurisdiction which is covered under question 3. However, anyone who has entered into a contract with the IRS to pay them, has to fulfill that contract unless he cancels all such contracts "for fraud".

How the IRS tricks its victims into becoming "liable"

IRS agants see it this way: By sending a 1040 tax return to the IRS, you 1) voluntarily assess yourself, you 2) acquiesce to IRS jurisdiction, and you 3) become "liable" for federal income tax; you 4) enter into a unilateral contract with them, which rebuttable for lack of full disclosure, which constitutes fraud.

When you open a bank account, on your signature card you sign something like, "Under penalty of perjury I certify that... [and] That the number shown on this form is my correct taxpayer identification number."

The signature card (without your knowledge) may also commit you to adhere to all current and future IRS regulations. Simply by opening a bank account you condemn yourself to being a "taxpayer" and you swear that your "social security number" is your "correct taxpayer identification number."

By understanding this, you can undo it, because these supposed "contracts" with the IRS aren't valid — they are rebuttable contracts.

2. Do all Americans have to file 1040 returns? If not, which Americans have to file?

Not all Americans have to file 1040 returns. Americans living and working outside federal jurisdiction (inside one of the 50 States) don't have to file. Those subject to federal jurisdiction (Washington DC, federal military installations, and U.S. territories like Puerto Rico, Guam, American Samoa, and the Virgin Islands) probably have to file. Once any American has filed a 1040 return, he or she must continue to file, unless he or she revokes the "election" to pay income taxes. This can be done verbally under penalty of perjury when necessary. See question #4.

3. What does the U.S. Constitution say about federal jurisdiction and how does this affect who is subject to federal income tax?

Two clauses in the Constitution define federal jurisdiction:

(a) Article I, Section 8, Clause 17: "The Congress shall have the power to exercise exclusive legislation, in all cases whatsoever, over such district (not exceeding ten miles square) as may, by cession of particular States, and the acceptance of Congress, become the seat of the Government of the United States; and to exercise like authority over all places purchased by the consent of the Legislature of the State in which the same shall be, for the erection of forts, magazines, arsenals, and other needful buildings..."

(b) Article IV, Section 3, Clause 2: "The Congress shall have the power to dispose of and make all needful rules and regulations respecting the territory or other property belonging to the United States..."

The territorial and legislative jurisdiction of the U.S. Congress extends to the ten square miles of Washington DC, military installations where States have explicitly ceded authority to the federal government, and U.S. Territories such as Puerto Rico, Guam, American Samoa, and the Virgin Islands. In accordance, IRS income taxes apply (if they apply at all) to people who live and/or work in these areas, or who work for the federal government.

4. Does the Internal Revenue Code specifically tell you how to terminate or revoke your "election" to pay federal income tax?

Section 6013(g)(4) TERMINATION OF ELECTION — An election under this subsection shall terminate at the earliest of the following times: (A) REVOCATION BY TAXPAYERS. — If either taxpayer revokes the election, as of the first taxable year for which the last day prescribed by law for filing the return of tax under chapter 1 has not yet occurred."

ORIGINALLY, MY ANSWER TO QUESTION 4. IMPLIED A "YES." HOWEVER, I WAS MISTAKEN. THE ABOVE IS REALLY AN "ELECTION" TO BE TREATED IN A DIFFERENT WAY BY THE IRS.

SO, THE CORRECT ANSWER TO QUESTION 4. IS "**NO!**" **The IRC does not tell you how...**

5. Why, in its literature, does the IRS consistently say that the federal income tax is based on "self-assessment and voluntary compliance?"

IRS literature often uses the terms "self-assessment" and "voluntary compliance." The reason for this is that senior IRS personnel know that the law does not require most Americans to file income tax returns. The income tax does not apply to most Americans unless they voluntarily (and knowingly!)

enter into a contract with the IRS. You <u>unknowingly</u> enter into a contract with the IRS by filling out, signing, and filing an income tax return . Once you have entered into such a contract it is not easy to get out of it. You can <u>put the burden on the IRS to</u> <u>"PROVE THEIR CLAIM"</u>.

Like all government agencies, the IRS has a mission. Its mission as published in the Federal Register of March 25, 1974, includes: **"The mission of the Service is to encourage and achieve the highest degree of voluntary compliance..."** Don't IRS Commissioners agree with the voluntary nature of federal income tax?

• "Each year American taxpayers voluntarily file their tax returns and make a special effort to pay the taxes they owe." — *Johnnie M. Walker, IRS Commissioner, 1971, Internal Revenue 1040 Booklet.*

• "Our tax system is based on individual self assessment and voluntary compliance." — *Mortimer Caplin, IRS Commissioner, 1975 Internal Revenue Audit Manual.*

• "In fairness to the millions of taxpayers who voluntarily file, report all their income and pay the tax due... ." — *Jerome Kurtz, IRS Commissioner, 1979 Internal Revenue Annual Report.*

• "The IRS's primary task is to collect taxes under a voluntary compliance system." — *Jerome Kurtz, IRS Commissioner, 1980 Internal Revenue Annual Report.*

• According to Alan Stang (*Taxscam: How The IRS Swindles You And What You Can Do About It*), Robert J. Brann, Chief of Technical Services Branch, IRS, Washington, D.C., wrote to a "gentleman in New York" on March 11, 1981:

> "In carrying out its responsibilities for administering the federal income tax laws, the Service encourages voluntary compliance by taxpayers. Voluntary compliance places on tax payers the initial responsibility for deciding whether under the law they are required to file returns, and the responsibility for paying any tax that may be due... "

• "Encourage and achieve the highest possible degree of voluntary compliance... " — *Harold M. Browning, IRS District Director, Hawaii, 1984.*

• "Let's not forget the delicate nature of the voluntary compliance tax system... " — *Lawrence Gibbs, IRS Commissioner, Las Vegas Review Journal, May 18, 1988.*

• "We don't want to lose voluntary compliance... We don't want to lose this gem of voluntary compliance." — *Fred Goldberg, IRS Commissioner, Money magazine, April, 1990.*

"Let me point this out now: Your income tax is 100 percent <u>voluntary</u> tax, and your liquor tax is 100 percent <u>enforced</u> tax. Now, the situation is as different as night and day." — *Dwight E. Avis, head of the Alcohol and Tobacco Tax Division, Bureau of Internal Revenue, testifying before the Ways and Means Committee during the Eighty-Third Congress in 1953.*

The tax return for a manufacturer of tobacco products says, "The information is mandatory by statute. (26 USC 5061, 5703)." <u>All mandatory tax returns mention penalties for not filing</u>, for example, the Alcoholic Beverage Tax Return states, "... punishable upon conviction by a fine of not more than $100,000.00... " Check your 1040 for the statute that says you must file, and the penalty for not filing — <u>you won't find them</u>.

Congress has a legal research branch called the <u>Congressional Research Service</u>.

A letter, dated June 26, 1989, from the office of Senator Daniel K. Inouye in Hawaii to a tax consultant Fred Ortiz states, that based on the research performed by the Congressional Research Service, **"There is no provision which specifically and unequivocally requires an individual to pay income taxes."** [Emphasis added]

Let me cite three court cases that seem to support the notion that the federal income tax is voluntary:

- "Our system of taxation is based upon voluntary assessment and payment, not upon distraint (seizure by distress)." — *Flora v. U.S., 362 U.S. 145, 176 (1959).*

- In case of any ambiguity of statutory construction, the doubt should be resolved in favor of the taxpayer, - not the government. — *Greyhound Corp. v. U.S., 495 F. 2d 863 (1974).*

- "The taxpayer must be liable for the tax. Tax liability is a condition precedent to the demand. Merely demanding payment, even repeatedly, does not cause liability... For the condition precedent of liability to be met, there must be a lawful assessment, either a voluntary one by the taxpayer, or one procedurally proper, by the IRS. Because this country's income tax system is based on voluntary assessment, rather than distraint [seizure by distress], the Service may assess the tax only in certain circumstances and in conformity with proper procedures." — *Bothke v. Fluor Engineers & Construction, Inc., Ninth Circuit (1983).*

"No person shall... be compelled in any criminal case to be a witness against himself." — 5th Amendment to the U.S. Constitution.

The Supreme Court ruled accordingly:

- The Fifth Amendment applies alike to criminal and civil proceedings." — *McCarthy v. Anderson, 266 U.S. 34.*

- "There can be no question that one who files a return under oath is a witness within the meaning of the [5th] Amendment." — *Sullivan v. U.S., 15 F2nd 809.*

- "The information revealed in the preparation and filing of an income tax return is, for 5th Amendment analysis, the testimony of a "witness" as that term is used herein." — *Garner v. U.S., 424 U.S. 648.*

6. What is the significance of the 1991 Supreme Court case, *Cheek vs. U.S.*? — *Cheek v. U.S. (No. 89-658; 1991 U.S. Lexis 348; 1991 WL 422 [U.S.])*

This Supreme Court case represents a major turning point for those seeking to defend their rights against the IRS. Prior to this case, many courts applied the so-called **"Cooley rule"** which was effectively used to prevent people from entering evidence for their own defence in tax cases. Typically, prosecutors would file preliminary ("in limine") motions **prohibiting defendants from entering evidence to defend themselves.** Thus most tax prosecutions occurred in farcical kangaroo courts where the defendants were not allowed to defend themselves!

The Cheek decision changed that. Among other things it found:

(a) Defendants may enter evidence in their defense.

(b) Defendants can provide a "good faith" defense: if they sincerely believed (no matter how irrational the belief) that they didn't have to file and pay income tax, then they can't be guilty of a crime.

7. What is the significance of the 1991 Fifth Circuit Court of Appeals case, *Ramon/Dolores Portillo vs. Internal Revenue*? — *Ramon and Dolores Portillo v. Commissioner of Internal Revenue. (932 F.2d 1128 (5th Cir., 1991) .*

The Cheek case was a severs blow to the IRS in **criminal** cases. The U.S. Court of Appeals of the Fifth Circuit likewise dealt a severe blow to the IRS in **civil** cases. The court effectively found that in the case of an IRS assessment of tax deficiency, the burden of proof shifts to the IRS. In other words, they have to prove that you owe them money.

8. Who are the people who have most to fear from the IRS?

8.1. Those who file tax returns are most at risk! Because of the ambiguities of the Internal Revenue

Code it is impossible to file a tax return without the IRS being able to nail you for filing a false return or committing perjury. — *"Come into my web said the spider to the fly."*

8.2. High-profile people like Leona Helmsley, Willie Nelson, and the late Red Foxx, who can be nailed as examples — providing wide media exposure — People who use IRS handmaiden lawyers and/or accountants to assist them in their tax affairs.

8.3. Tax protestors who stop filing and/or paying without properly terminating their contracts with the IRS.

8.4. The people who have least to fear from the IRS are those who have never entered into a contract with the IRS, those who know the weaknesses of the IRS, those who have properly "untaxed" themselves, and those who have organized their personal affairs so they don't own any assets and don't have any bank accounts the IRS or other government looters can seize.

It is important that you realize that the Internal Revenue Code is so complex and convoluted that nobody can understand it. This means that whatever tax return you file can be "proved" by the IRS to constitute fraud and perjury.

"Well, it's a system so utterly complex and ultimately inexplicable that half the time the tax professionals themselves aren't sure what the rules are — a system that even Albert Einstein is said to have admitted he couldn't begin to fathom. You know, it's said that his hair didn't look that way until after he experienced his first tax form." — *Ronald Reagan, 1985.*

Every year since 1987 *Money* magazine has run a contest in which 50 tax preparers complete the federal income tax return for a hypothetical family. In 1988 there were ten correct returns, in 1989 two, in 1990 one, and in 1991 zero. For the 1991 tax year the "target tax" was $26,619 - the tax amount for a correct tax return. Not one of the professional tax preparers got it right. At the low extreme, one tax preparer calculated the tax due as $16,219. She spent 25 hours on the job and charged a fee of $750. At the high extreme, another professional tax preparer calculated the tax due as $46,564. It took him 40 hours and he charged $3,000.

The contestants presumably fancied themselves as expert tax preparers, and did their utmost to win first prize. They consisted mostly of professional CPAs and former IRS agents. If you take your papers and records to two "professional tax preparers," one might calculate your tax as $16,000, and the other as $46,000! Need I say any more?

Note that if you had hired any of these professionals to prepare your tax return, the result could have been prosecution for fraud and perjury. Not one of them got it right

9. **What should you do in order to understand the IRS and to safely defend against it?**

File your complaint under **Title 15** - **United States Fair Debt Collection Practices Act** — instead of under **Title 26** - **Internal Revenue Code**.

The non-federal **Internal Revenue Service** is a private, for-profit **debt collection agency** for the private, non-federal **Federal Reserve Bank**.

IRS NOTICE OF LEVY (OR LIEN) PERTAINS TO ESTATE TAX - NOT 1040 TAX

A Privacy Act transcript has codes on it just like an Individual Master File (IMF) does. The codes on it are almost the same as the IMF codes, except for one big difference between the two that is very revealing, involving Code No. 582.

The IRS has a pocket transaction code guide that identifies what all these code numbers mean and it shows here that Code No. 582 stands for "lien filed".

But on the Privacy Act transcript under Code No. 582, instead of saying "lien filed" it says "election of estate carryover basis on 2032(a) valuation".

Well, that doesn't sound much like a tax lien.

The IRS Notice of Federal Tax Levy or Lien always has the designation "1040" for the "type of tax". In other words, "1040" is the type of tax that the IRS claims a person is liable for.

This "1040" is a Form Number (i.e., Form 1040) not a specific income or other tax.

There is no such thing as a "Form 1040 tax".

So, what specific tax is the accused liable for?

The "1040" that appears on a Notice of Levy, for the type of tax, does not pertain to Form 1040; it pertains to Section 040 of the tax code.

Section 1040 under Subtitle A of Title 26 says:

Section 1040 - Transfer of certain farm, etc. real property

If the executor of the estate of any decedent transfers to a qualified heir (within the meaning of section 2032A(e)(1)) any property with respect to which an election was made under section 2032A, then gain on such transfer shall be recognized to the estate only to the extent that, on the date of such transfer, the fair market value of such property exceeds the value of such property for purposes of chapter 11

(determined without regard to section 2032A)

Section 2032A says "valuation of certain farm, etc. real property" as does Section 1040, but now an important change takes place. Instead of talking about something under Subtitle A of the tax code, it is talking about something under Subtitle B of the tax code.

Well, Subtitle B pertains to estate and gift taxes, not income taxes.

Section 2032A - Valuation of certain farm, etc. real property
(a) Value based on use under which property qualifies
(1) General rule. If-
(A) the decedent was (at the time of his death) a citizen or resident of the United States, and
(B) the executor elects the application of this section and files the agreement referred to in subsection (d)(2).

Thus, the 1040 listed as the "type of tax" on the Notice of Levy (or Lien) is not referencing a Subtitle A income tax; it's referencing a Subtitle B estate tax.

Sections 2001 & 2002 of the tax code, under Subtitle B, talk about two things: the imposition of an estate tax, and the liability for its payment by the executor.

Section 2001 - Imposition and rate of tax
(a) Imposition. A tax is hereby imposed on the transfer of the taxable estate of every decedent who is a citizen or resident of the United States.

Section 2002 - Liability for payment
The tax imposed by this chapter shall be paid by the executor.

The Notice of Federal Tax Levy or Lien is on an alleged estate and they consider you as the executor of the estate.

Since an estate tax is imposed upon an executor under Section 1040 of the tax code, they consider you liable to pay it.

However, In order for you to become the executor of an estate, somebody has to die.

The IRS has misled people into thinking that their Notice of Levy (or Lien) pertains to some kind of Form 1040 tax; yet in reality it pertains to the Section 1040 tax described under Section 2032A of the tax code, which is an estate tax that has nothing to do with Subtitle A income taxes.

If they say it refers to Form 1040, then it brings us back to the question of what specific tax, since Form 1040 is not a tax?

So challenge the IRS to explain :

1) who died; 2) when did you became an executor of an estate; and, 3) whose estate is it; etc.?

Question:

Does the IRS see you, **John Doe** — *the real, non-corporate, flesh and blood man* — **as dead, and the State** — *the corporate United States* — **as the Executive Director, Administrator, and Beneficiary of your trust estate** — *the JOHN DOE TRUST ESTATE* — **that the State created in your name** — *via your birth Certificate after you were delivered to the State by your mother and the doctor* — **after you were born.**

And your fictional strawman, JOHN DOE — *who is a Citizen of the corporate United States having been created thereby* — **as the Trustee** (*of your trust estate*) **who manages the business** (*of your trust estate*) **producing income for your trust estate, to be transferred by the Executor** (*of your trust estate*) **to the the Beneficiary** (*of your trust estate*) **each year** — *because of your death that the State arranged via your birth Certificate when your doctor and your mother delivered you to the State shortly after you were born* — **as a 1040 Estate tax to the State?**

Answer:

We Plaintiffs believe so...

"1040" is Section 1040 of the tax code, not Form 1040. There's just too much of a coincidence.

The IRS wants Payors to use all these 1099s, W-2s and W-4s with respect to payments that they pay out to others not knowing that each of these forms are designated for estate tax purposes and now we find out that their Notice of Federal Tax Lien pertains to an estate tax lien?

The IRS trying to seize all kinds of property when their only authority to do so is for stamp taxes; it is just another twisting of things.

According to the IRS, the IRS must have a lien in place before they can impose a levy, as well. Even so, what kind of tax it is that they are trying to collect?

Trap these people into admitting the type of tax the Notice of Levy pertains to.

LEGAL INFORMATION INSTITUTE (LII) OF CORNELL UNIVERSITY

Thank you for wanting to learn more about the LII. We are a small research, engineering, and editorial group housed at the Cornell Law School in Ithaca, NY. Our collaborators include publishers, legal scholars, computer scientists, government agencies, and other groups and individuals that promote open access to law, worldwide.

Here you can learn about all the things we do to ensure that the law remains free and open to everyone.

Mission

We are a not-for-profit group that believes everyone should be able to read and understand the laws that govern them, without cost. We carry out this vision by:

- Publishing law online, for free.

- Creating materials that help people understand law.

- Exploring new technologies that make it easier for people to find the law.

Learn how we fulfill our mission.

History

The Legal Information Institute (LII) was founded in 1992 by co-directors Thomas R. Bruce and Peter W. Martin (now Director and Director Emeritus, respectively). Its work is supported by the National Center for Automated Information Research, a growing number of corporate sponsors, and the Keck Foundation through grants and funded joint studies.

The LII publishes electronic versions of core materials in numerous areas of the law, both on the web and in other electronic products. They range from the Constitution to the U.S. Code, from Supreme Court decisions to the Code of Federal Regulations. It maintains this Internet site and its many resources. It builds software tools assisting Internet users and publishers. And through workshops and consultation it works to aid others who want to explore the full potential of electronic publication and communication.

The LII is known internationally as a leading "law-not-com" provider of public legal information. We offer all opinions of the United States Supreme Court handed down since 1992, together with over 600 earlier decisions selected for their historic importance, over a decade of opinions of the New York Court of Appeals, and the full United States Code. We also publish important secondary sources: libraries in two important areas (legal ethics and social security) and a series of "topical" pages that serve as concise explanatory guides and Internet resource listings for roughly 100 areas of law.

Search engines and ranking systems identify the LII as the most linked-to web resource in the field of law (see, for example, Google). Sites ranging from CSPAN to Fedlaw to the Dow Jones Business Directory, as well as numerous off-line references, e.g., Web Feet, the New York Times, and The National Jurist (4/2000), recommend starting with the LII for law.

Want to learn more?

You can watch a short video about the LII, read testimonials from our users, and meet the LII Staff.

What We Do

Most of our publishing efforts go into to producing and maintaining the extensive legal collections on this web site. In 2011, we partnered with eLangdell to produce eBooks of the Federal Rules, the first three volumes of a growing collection. Soon, you will find LII-powered collections available for smartphone and tablet use. As the first law site on the Internet, we are proud to lend our expertise to new LIIs that develop in all parts of the world. Currently, we helping to build LIIs in Africa.

Complaint and Motion for Summary Judgement or Jury Trial

Helping Understanding

The law is a complex and complicated system of knowledge that is more difficult to find and understand that it should be. While we are not permitted to offer legal advice, we try to develop systems that allow users from outside the legal profession to more easily access and understand the laws that govern them. Our Wex Legal Encyclopedia includes hundred of definitions and explanations of legal topics. The LII Supreme Court Bulletin keeps you apprised of all pending Supreme Court cases and alerts you with the decisions as soon as they are available. LII Announce is our blog that lets you know about what's new at the LII and in the world of legal information and research. And if you are a law student or researcher, you should try our Jureeka! browser plug-in that turns legal citations in web pages into direct links to the relevant item in the LII collections.

Exploring Technologies

The LII is proud to host visiting researchers who come here to learn and perform research that will help the spread of the free-law movement around the world. The LII also partners with our colleagues at Cornell Law School and Cornell University to put our technical knowledge to use on other problems facing society. You can learn more about our research on our forthcoming research pages, or explore VoxPopuLII, our blog for new voices in legal information research.

How the LII is Funded

20% of our funding is contributed by generous people like you who believe that law should be freely available to everyone. All of your donations go directly toward supporting the LII itself. Please donate to LII.

20% of our funding is provided through online sponsorships, online advertising, and projects with partner organizations (like our Lawyer Directory and eBooks) that help generate funds for the LII. We also obtain grants from government and non-governmental organizations, but these funds go directly to support the research goals and technology needs affiliated with the specific grant.

60% of our funding comes as direct support from Cornell Law School, which also provides us with some administrative apparatus and office space in the Jane Foster Tower at Myron Taylor Hall.

How we use funds

The main expense in running a website is not technology, even on a site that offers nearly 500,000 pages to 15 million unique visitors every year. Instead, more than 80% of our budget goes to salaries for our small staff, and to stipends for the law and computer science students who work with us. Almost all the remainder is spent on computing facilities, which we tailor to demand using cloud-computing technology. Less than 5% goes to administrative overhead.

Because our core staff is small and our activity level is high, it is hard to tell you precisely how this money is spent. How much of the time that Dan Nagy spent working on a server should be allocated to the WEX legal encyclopedia? To the collection of Supreme Court decisions? How often do Dave Shetland's code libraries get used for the Code of Federal Regulations, and how often for the US Code? How many red pencils did Sara Frug use up editing the Federal Rules? These are hard questions to answer, and maybe not so important so long as you understand that nearly all of your money buys talent. We try to apply that talent as effectively and efficiently as we can.

How to Contact the LII

Before you contact us, please understand that **the LII cannot and does not provide legal advice or interpretations of the law. We are prohibited by law from doing so.** We will not answer or reply to requests for legal advice, so please do not ask.

If you need legal advice, you can find an attorney in our lawyer directory, or you can ask your question to our partner, JustAnswer, who may be able to assist you. The JustAnswer link is provided as a convenience to LII users. JustAnswer is a separate company with its own pricing and service terms. LII is not responsble for information provided by the JustAnswer service.

To send questions or comments about this site or an LII service via email:

Send email to the LII: help@liicornell.org

Our mailing address is:

Legal Information Institute, Cornell Law School, 477 Myron Taylor Hall, Ithaca, NY 14853.

15 USC Chapter 41, Subchapter V - DEBT COLLECTION PRACTICES

- § 1692 . Congressional findings and declaration of purpose
- §1692a . Definitions
- **§1692b . Acquisition of location information**
- **§1692c . Communication in connection with debt collection**
- **§1692d . Harassment or abuse**
- **§1692e . False or misleading representations**
- **§1692f . Unfair practices**
- **§1692g . Validation of debts**
- §1692h . Multiple debts
- §1692i . Legal actions by debt collectors
- §1692j . Furnishing certain deceptive forms
- §1692k . Civil liability
- **§1692l . Administrative enforcement**
- §1692m . Reports to Congress by the Bureau; views of other Federal agencies
- §1692n . Relation to State laws

- §1692o . Exemption for State regulation
- §1692p . Exception for certain bad check enforcement programs operated by private entities
- §1692. Congressional findings and declaration of purpose
- §1692a. Definitions
- §1692b. Acquisition of location information
- §1692c. Communication in connection with debt collection
- §1692d. Harassment or abuse
- §1692e. False or misleading representations
- §1692f. Unfair practices
- §1692g. Validation of debts
- §1692h. Multiple debts
- §1692i. Legal actions by debt collectors
- §1692j. Furnishing certain deceptive forms
- §1692k. Civil liability
- §1692l. Administrative enforcement
- §1692m. Reports to Congress by the Commission; views of other Federal agencies
- §1692n. Relation to State laws
- §1692o. Exemption for State regulation
- §1692p. Exception for certain bad check enforcement programs operated by private entities

The table below lists the classification updates, since **Jan. 7, 2011**, for the contained sections. If there are multiple sections, they are presented in section number order (original document order).

The most recent Classification Table update that we have noticed was **Friday, April 6, 2012**

An empty table indicates that we see no relevant changes listed in the classification tables. If you suspect that our system may be missing something, please double-check with the Office of the Law Revision Counsel.

How To Use

Multiple entries for a section are listed most recent first, within the section.

The Session Year indicates which session of Congress was responsible for the changes classified. The Congress number forms the first part of the Public Law number; each Congress has two sessions.

Abbreviations used in the Description of Change column:

- An empty field implies a standard amendment.

- "new" means a new section or new note, or all new text of an existing section or note.

- "nt" means note.

- "nt [tbl]" means note [table].

- "prec" means preceding.

- "fr" means a transfer from another section.

- "to" means a transfer to another section.

- "omitted" means the section is omitted.

- "repealed" means the section is repealed.

- "nt ed change" and "ed change" - See the

- Editorial Classification Change Table [pdf].

The Public Law field is linked to the development of the law in the Thomas system at the Library of Congress.

The Statutes at Large field is linked to the text of the law, in the context of its volume of the Statutes at Large, at the Government Printing Office. Please note that it takes a while for these pages to get posted, so for very recent legislation, you need to look at the "enrolled" version at the Thomas site.

The Statutes at Large references have been rendered in the format used as page numbers in the Public Law web pages to which we link, to facilitate copy-paste into browser "find on this (web) page" tools. We are still working on a more direct link facility.

For serious comparison work, we suggest copying all or a portion of the Public Law text into your favorite text editor, for convenient content traversal and window control.

Sections with change type "new" are a special case, still under development. All are now listed, at the title level only.

You will find that occassionally a specific update you notice in a Public Law listed in a classification table will already have made it into the Code. We assume this is an artifact of the LRC edit process. The LII does not edit the LRC content.

top General Reference

Refer to the LRC (Law Revision Council) for explanations about the US Code from the folks who put it all together.

You can look for information about what it is and is not, which titles are *positive law*, the schedule of Supplements, etc. Under download you can find the source data we use here (GPO locator files), as well as, PDF files that look just like the paper books (these may be rather large).

Refer to the Thomas site for changes that have not yet made it into the classification tables.

Epistle to the Americans I

What you don't know about the Income Tax
Authored by David E. Robinson

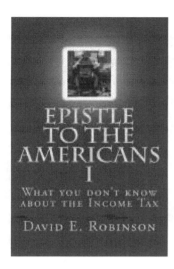

Under the Supreme Court's "Collective Entity Rule" named in IRS 7701(a) is a"person" created on paper, a "strawman," a legal person that has no constitutional rights. ... (1 AMERICANS 40:1)

The difference between a "person" who has no rights and a natural person is that . . . "The individual may stand upon his constitutional rights as a citizen. ... He owes no duty to the State, since he receives nothing therefrom, beyond the protection of his life and property. His rights ... can only be taken from him by due process of law and in accordance with the Constitution." (1 AMERICANS 40:2-3)

Publication Date:	Sep 09 2009
ISBN/EAN13:	1448698820 / 9781448698820
Page Count:	138
Binding Type:	US Trade Paper
Trim Size:	5.5" x 8.5"
Language:	English
Color:	Black and White

Related Categories: Education / Genera

https://www.createspace.com/3398018

Commercial Law Applied

Learn To Play The Game

Authored by David E. Robinson

The principles, maxims and precepts of Commercial Law are eternal, unchanging and unchangeable. They are expressed in the Bible, both in the Old Testament and in the New.

The law of commerce — unchanged for thousands of years — forms the underlying foundation of all law on this planet; and for governments around the world. It is the law of nations, and of everything that human civilization is built upon.

This is why Commercial Law is so powerful.

When you operate at the level of Commercial Law, by these precepts, nothing that is of inferior statute can overturn or change it, or abrogate it, or meddle with it. It is the fundamental source of all authority, power and functional reality.

Publication Date:	Aug 20 2012
ISBN/EAN13:	1478390352 / 9781478390350
Page Count:	138
Binding Type:	US Trade Paper
Trim Size:	5.5" x 8.5"
Language:	English
Color:	Black and White

Related Categories: Education / Adult & Continuing Education

https://www.createspace.com/3960715

Be The One

To Execute Your Trust
Authored by David E. Robinson

Presumptions? or Facts!

The State operates on presumptions. Courts operate on presumptions. But what binds me to their presumptions?

Where's the contract? What obligations in the contract am I allegedly bound to perform? Did I agree to it? Was the contract valid? Was mutual consideration exchanged? What type of consideration was exchanged? What is in the contract that I am supposed to perform? Was I aware of the contract? Was the contract fully disclosed? Did I sign the contract with my autograph in ink?

Statutory laws are public servant codes for society's slaves; for agents of government. We're all presumed to be employees and servants of the state.

But, we're servants of God instead; students of the earth, charged with its cultivation and care.

Publication Date:	Jul 05 2012
ISBN/EAN13:	1478144831 / 9781478144830
Page Count:	118
Binding Type:	US Trade Paper
Trim Size:	5.5" x 8.5"
Language:	English
Color:	Black and White

Related Categories: Law / Contracts

https://www.createspace.com/3921716

Other Publications

Untold History Of America: Let The Truth Be Told
http://tinyurl.com/bu9kjjc

Debtocracy: & Odious Debt Explained
http://tinyurl.com/cooqzuz

New Beginning Study Course: Connect The Dots And See
http://tinyurl.com/cxpk42p

Monitions of a Mountain Man: Manna, Money, & Me
http://tinyurl.com/cusgcqs

Maine Street Miracle: Saving Yourself And America
http://tinyurl.com/d4yktlw

Reclaim Your Sovereignty: Take Back Your Christian Name
http://tinyurl.com/cf5taxh

Gun Carry In The USA: Your Right To Self-defence
http://tinyurl.com/cdn3y3y

Climategate Debunked: Big Brother, Main Stream Media
http://tinyurl.com/d6gy2xz

Epistle to the Americans I: What you don't know about The Income Tax
http://tinyurl.com/d99ujzm

Epistle to the Americans II: What you don't know about American History
http://tinyurl.com/cnyghyz

Epistle to the Americans III: What you don't know about Money
http://tinyurl.com/cp8nrh8

NESARA I & II: National Economic Security and Reformation Act
I: http://tinyurl.com/c8u42q6
II: http://tinyurl.com/848mqag

History of Banking: An Asian Perspective
http://tinyurl.com/7oxjwft

The People's Voice: Former Arizona Sheriff Richard Mack
http://tinyurl.com/d62fyg3

Asset Protection: Pure Trust Organizations
http://tinyurl.com/btrjfqp

The Matrix As It Is: A Different Point Of View
http://tinyurl.com/87pbtom

From Debt To Prosperity: 'Social Credit' Defined
http://tinyurl.com/c4r577x

Give Yourself Credit: Money Doesn't Grow On Trees
http://tinyurl.com/d9mf5yt

My Home Is My Castle: Beware Of The Dog
http://tinyurl.com/bmzxc2n

Commercial Redemption: The Hidden Truth
http://tinyurl.com/d9etg7w

Hardcore Redemption-In-Law: Commercial Freedom And Release
http://tinyurl.com/cl65vrz

Oil Beneath Our Feet: America's Energy Non-Crisis
http://tinyurl.com/btlzqxf

Plaintiffs repeat, reallege, and incorporate herein, by reference, Exhibit A

Complaint and Motion for Summary Judgement or Jury Trial

CUMBERLAND COUNTY SHERIFF'S OFFICE

36 County Way
Portland, Maine 04102
207.774.1444 ext. 2115
www.cumberlandso.org

SHERIFF / CITIZEN COMPLAINT FORM

Name of the Party Accused:	Control Number:

EXHIBIT A

Complainant's Name:	Home Address:	Home Telephone:
David E. Robinson	3 Linnell Circle Brunswick, Maine	798-4695
Witnesses / Other Complainants: F. William Messier	Home Address: 40 Tower Lane Brunswick, Maine	Home Telephone: 729-6667
Witnesses / Other Complainants:	Home Address:	Home Telephone:

Date / Time of Incident:	Location of Incident:
See Complaint, pages 2-19	Brunswick, Cumberland County, Maine

Nature of the Complaint:

Conspiracy to commit Fraud and unlawful seizure of personal property

Cumberland County Sheriff's Office

THE COMPLAINT

Conspiracy to commit Fraud and unlawful seizure of personal property through third parties by a private unregistered debt collection agency of the non-federal Federal Reserve Bank.

Wm. Francis Messier (a.k.a. Bill Messier) owns the highest property in Brunswick, Maine, in Cumberland County, on which 6 telecommunication towers are placed, 4 of which serve 15 paying customers. The Accused are stealing his lease receipts from his 15 customers without his right to due process of law and refuse to respond to his lawful demands.

THE ACCUSED

Joline P. Hendershot, INTERNAL REVENUE SERVICE, 217 Main Street, Lewiston, ME 04240

Patrick Frie, INTERNAL REVENUE SERVICE, 220 Maine Mall Road, South Portland, ME 04106

Jason S. Rogers, Special Agent, Criminal Investigation, DEPARTMENT OF THE TREASURY, INTERNAL REVENUE SERVICE, 220 Maine Mall Road, South Portland, ME 04106

PREFACE

Commerce consists of a mode of interacting and resolving disputes whereby all matters are executed under oath by sworn affidavit executed under the penalty of perjury as true, correct, and complete.

An affidavit is one's solemn expression of his truth. When you issue an affidavit you get the power of an affidavit. You also incur the liability involved.

An unrebutted affidavit becomes judgment in commerce. Proceedings consist of contests of commercial affidavits wherein the unrebutted points in the end stand as truth to which judgment of law applies.

Commercial Law is pre-judicial non-judical.

A claim can be satisfied only through (1) rebuttal by affidavit point by point; (2) resolution by jury; or (3) payment or performance of the claim.

The conflict between Commercial Affidavits gives a clean basis for resolving disputes.

UNREBUTTED POINTS

1 • There is no law that requires most Americans to file an individual tax return.

2 • The Internal Revenue Service (IRS) wasn't created by an act of Congress.

3 • The Public Salary Tax Act (26 USC 1) was passed in 1930 to impose a tax upon the income of federal employees, U.S. citizens [of the District of Columbia] and non-resident aliens.

4 • The Public Salary Tax Act of 1939 did not apply to Citizens of the forty-eight (48) now fifty (50) States.

5 • Congress passed the Victory Tax Act of 1942, after Pearl Harbor was bombed by Japan on December 7, 1941 to raise money to support an Army, in accordance with Article I, Section 8, Clause 12 of the Constitution of the United States of America:

6 • Article I, Section 8, Clause 12 states that "Congress shall have Power ... To raise and support Armies, but no Appropriation of Money to that Use shall be for a longer term that two Years."

7 • IRS 1040 Forms only apply to government employees, citizens and residents of the District of Columbia, and non resident aliens.

8 • The Bureau of Internal Revenue sent out 1040 Forms in 1942 to the general public in the forty-eight states, even though the Victory Tax Act of 1942 didn't apply to the general public in the forty-eight states.

9 • Most people voluntarily filed a Form 1040 in 1942, 1943, and in 1944 not realizing that direct taxes were not allowed according to the U.S. Constitution and that the Victory Tax Act of 1942 was an extension of the Public Salary Tax Act of 1939 which referred to the public salaries of public government employees and not the general public.

10 • Congress repealed the Victory Tax Act of 1942 on May 29, 1944 but the news media did not publicize the repeal.

11 • The Bureau of Internal Revenue mass mailed 1040 Forms to the general public in 1945 just to see what would happen.

12 • The public filled out the 1040 Forms and mailed them in along with their checks thinking that the Victory Tax Act was mandatory in the then forty-eight (48) States without knowing that the Act had been repealed.

13 • The Bureau of Internal Revenue has continued the Fraud on the Citizens of the forty-eight (48) now (50) States and has continued to fraudulently send out Form 1040's each and every year ever since.

14 • The mainstream media are accessories after the fact to the IRS Fraud.

15 • The name of the "Public Salary Tax Act of 1939" was changed to the "Internal Revenue Code" (IRC) and amended in 1953 and 1987.

16 • The "Internal Revenue Code" (IRC) only applies to the District of Columbia and the federal territories and possessions.

17 • There is no authority for the IRS to operate within the fifty (50) states of the Union.

18 • The Internal Revenue Bureau (IRB) and the Internal Revenue Service (IRS) were not created by an act of Congress.

19 • The Internal Revenue Bureau (IRB) and the Internal Revenue Service (IRS) are not agencies of the U.S. Department of the Treasury nor of the federal government

20 • The Internal Revenue Bureau (IRB) and the Internal Revenue Service (IRS are agencies of the Department of the Treasury of Puerto Rico.

21 • All Revenue Agents and Officers work as employees of the Department of the Treasury of the Commonwealth of Puerto Rico.

22 • The Internal Revenue Service does not have any jurisdiction or authority over a Sovereign Citizen nor state to enforce the unlawful provisions of the Internal Revenue Code.

23 • The "Internal Revenue Service" has no legal jurisdiction in any of the fifty (50) States of the Union of American States.

24 • The IRS is perpetrating the greatest income tax fraud on the Citizens of America that this country has ever ignorantly not seen.

25 • The IRS deals with a person's strawman under Administrative law according to Title 26

26 • The IRS is a debt collection agency for the non-federal Federal Reserve Bank and operates under Title 15 instead of Title 26.

27 • Title 15 comes under the FAIR DEBT COLLECTIONS PRACTICES ACT (FDCPA) and deals with natural persons who have human and constitutional rights under Private law.

28 • The IRS is a private for-profit debt collection agency for the non-federal Federal Reserve Bank.

29 • The IRS is a private for profit debt collection agency under the Legislative branch of the government which is Private law.

30 • When dealing with the IRS under Title 15 a person is seen to be a natural person who can invoke the private protections and rights of Constitutional law.

31 • The Accused are acting under wrongfully assumed Authority and Powers and under the pretense and color of office, laws, and title.

32 • The Accused have been given Notice of Wm. Messier's ownership of real and personal property stolen, embezzled, converted and/or purloined, by and through certain illegal and unlawful acts including but not limited to wrongful issuance of 20 or more NOTICES OF LEVY issued by

JOLINE P. HENDERSHOT between April 15, 2012 and today that are effecting the false impression of actual LEVIES warranted by a judge.

33 • The above claim 32 was effected by out of court procedures and modes under the appearance of legitimacy to coerce fifteen (15) or more customers of FRANCIS WILLIAM MESSIER into illegally and unlawfully seizing, stealing, retaining and being in unlawful possession, custody and/or control of approximately $50,000.00 "Dollars" so far which was/is lawfully payable to Francis William Messier domiciled on the land at 40 Tower Lane, near Brunswick, Maine 04011, in the County of Cumberland, within the territorial jurisdiction of the Republic of Maine.

34 • The Accused and their Officers, Employer, Agents and/or Representatives are "agents of a foreign Principal" pursuant to 22 USCS 611.

35 • The Accused and their Officers, Employer, Agents and/or Representatives are directed, controlled, financed, subsidized and/or compensated for aiding, abetting, counseling, commanding, representing, and procuring the gathering of information, soliciting, collecting, disbursing, dispensing money, currency, or other things of value for or in interest of (A) "The United Nations" whose seat of government is in New York City, New York (22 USCS 287, 61 Stat. 3416); (B) "The Association" (22 USCS 284 et seq.); (C) "The Bank" and (D) "The Fund" (22 USCS 286 et seq.); and their subsidiary artificial beings pursuant to Public Law 94-564, Public Law 86-147, Public Law 89-369, Public Law 93-83, 87 Stat. 197, et cetera. (See also: 22 USCS 263(a); 22 USCS 285(g); 22 U.S.C.S. 287(j); 26 USCS 6103(k)(4); Executive Order 10033.)

36 • Internal Revenue Service Agents are in fact engaged in inter-agency, international stipulations, agreements and commerce with "The Association" and/or the "International Bank for Reconstruction And Development" and its many-faceted subsidiary, artificial beings, pursuant to "Treasury Delegation Order No. 91 (Rev. 1)," and "Service Agreements described in paragraph IV, of the General Agreement between the Treasury Department and the Agency for International Development, dated February 14, 1966" (Bretton Woods Agreement; 22 U.S.C.S. 284 et seq.).

37 • The character of "The Association," "The Bank," "The Fund," and the Governor of the Fund a/k/a Secretary of the Treasury (See: 22 USCS 286(a)), his associates, delegates, officers, employees, representatives, servants, and/or agents, being the real parties in interest, were and are now subject to Article III, Section 2, Clauses 1 and 2, as a matter of supreme Law, and/or Act of Congress, 22 USCS 286(g).

38 • The acts of the Accused and/or authorization of acts are acts committed under Letters of Marque issued on behalf of THEIR Foreign Principal and its artificial Organizations, and clearly in excess of the express and conditional, delegated and vested Powers and Authority, as established by the Ordained Constitution for the Union of several States of the United States of America.

39 • Francis W. Messier has RIGHTFULLY DEMANDED the immediate return of the above stated

sum of $50,000.00 "Dollars" pursuant to 18 USCS 645, and all other property and rights to property as stolen, confiscated and expropriated in violation of Act of Congress, coded Title 18 USCS 654 and 241; and under authority of the Declaration of Independence; the Ordained Constitution for the united States of America (1787), Article I Section 10, Clause I; Act of Congress, coded Title 31 USCS 314, 321, 5112; Public Law 93-110, Article IV, Section 2; and Amendments I, IV, V, VI, IX, and X.

40 • Francis W. Messier has RIGHTFULLY DEMANDED the same said property be returned to his personal care, custody, possession and control, to the address given above from which it was taken, seized, stolen and confiscated by his customers under the orders of the Accused.

41 • Due to the residency and collateral fact that the Accused and/or their Foreign Principals, Organizations, Associations, Officers, Employees, Representatives, Servants, or other Individuals acting under their direction and control, are incapable of maintaining the integrity of the de jure, Lawful, Constitutional Monetary System of the de jure Union of several Republican States of the United States of America, and are not heirs in Law or by birthright, i.e. Posterity, and have caused grievous harm, damage and injury under pretense and color of law, and are in breach of numerous legal duties imposed upon our Public Offices, they (the Accused) by Law are barred, estopped and precluded, under the "Clean Hands doctrine," and "Public Policy," from making any claim of right, title, or interest thereon. (See: 18 USCS 1001).

42 • The letterhead of the Accused's NOTICES OF LEVY and their business cards state that the notices are documents of "Department of the Treasury - Internal Revenue Service"; however, the Department of Justice letterhead says: "U.S. Department of Justice - Tax Division".

43 • The Accused are not officers or employees or assignees of the United States Government.

44 • The IRS is not an organization within the United States Department of the Treasury.

45 • There is no organic Act creating the IRS as a lawful organization.

46 • The IRS is a collection agency working for foreign banks and operating out of Puerto Rico under color of the Federal Alcohol Administration (FAA).

47 • The FAA was promptly declared unconstitutional inside the 50 States by the U.S. Supreme Court in the case of U.S. v. Constantine, 296 U.S. 287 (1935) because Prohibition had been repealed.

48 • There is no legal authority for the IRS to establish offices inside the 50 States of the Union.

49 • The IRS can not legally show "Department of the Treasury" on their outgoing mail.

50 • The U.S. Department of Justice does not have power of attorney to represent the IRS in federal court.

51 • The IRS is domiciled in Puerto Rico.

52 • The so-called 14th and 16th amendments were not properly ratified.

53 • There are no statutes that create a specific liability for federal income taxes, except for government employees pursuant to the Public Salary Tax Act.

54 • A federal regulation can not create a specific liability when no specific liability is created by the corresponding statute.

55 • An administrative agency can not create a criminal offense or any liability not sanctioned by the lawmaking authority.

56 • Federal regulations create an income tax liability for only TWO classes of people: federal citizens and federal employees.

57 • One can be a state citizen without being a federal citizen.

58 • State citizens are nonresident aliens with respect to the municipal jurisdiction of Congress, i.e. the federal zone.

59 • A "withholding agent" is one who is authorized by an employee to withhold part of his wages.

60 • The payroll officer does not have "permission" or "power of attorney" to withhold taxes from workers who do not authorize or "allow" withholding by knowingly, intentionally, and voluntarily signing an IRS Form W4.

61 • A properly executed Form W4 creates the presumption that the worker wishes to be treated as if he were an "employee" of the federal government.

62 • A "Withholding Exemption Certificate" can be personally created and executed as an alternative to Form W4 in lieu of a Form W4.

63 • Filing a Form W4 is not mandatory for workers who are not "employed" by the federal government.

64 • Protesting the claims of the IRS is not "tax evasion".

65 • Only "taxpayers" can be found guilty of "tax evasion."

66 • Corporations chartered by the 50 States of the Union are technically "foreign" corporations with respect to the IRC.

67 • Congress has no authority to create a national corporation.

68 • The IRS does not require a Notary Public to notarize a taxpayer's signature on a Form 1040 even though Congress mandates that written verifications must be executed under penalty of perjury and a Notary Public as a witness to one's signature.

69 • The terms "United States" and "United States of America" do not refer to the same entity.

70 • Verifications executed "outside the "United States" (the federal zone) are executed "inside the States of the Union.

71 • The term "United States" has multiple legal meanings; geographical, political, territorial.

72 • The term "income" is not defined in the IRC.

73 • The term "income" means the profit or gain derived from corporate activity under the corporate privilege of limited liability.

74 • Income tax provisions do not constitute Municipal law.

75 • Municipal law is law that is enacted to govern the internal affairs of a sovereign State.

76 • Municipal law in legal circles is also known as Private International Law.

77 • The Internal Revenue Code is not a Municipal Revenue Code.

78 • The State of Maine is not mentioned in any of the federal income tax statutes.

79 • Congress has no authority to exercise a power that is not enumerated in the U.S. Constitution.

80 • No federal income tax statute has any force or effect within the State of Maine.

81 • Vagueness is sufficient grounds for concluding that the entire IRS Code is unconstitutional, null, and void.

82 • The entire IRS Code is unconstitutional, null, and void for violating our fundamental Right to know the nature and cause of any accusation as guaranteed by the Sixth Amendment in the Bill of Rights.

83 • Title 26 of the United States Code was never enacted into positive law.

84 • Federal courts are not authorized to prosecute income tax crimes.

85 • Constitutional District Courts of the United States ("DCUS") are not the same as legislative United States District Courts ("USDC").

86 • Federal judges are not required to pay income taxes on their pay.

87 • Federal judges routinely rule in favor of the IRS because they fear the retaliation that might result from ruling against the IRS.

88 • Federal grand juries can not issue valid indictments against illegal tax protesters.

89 • IRS agents tamper with federal grand juries by misrepresenting themselves, under oath, as lawful employees and "special agents" of the federal government.

90 • IRS agents tamper with federal grand juries by acting as if "income" is everything that "comes in"; when there is no such definition anywhere in the IR Code.

91 • Bank signature cards constitute competent waivers of their customers' fundamental rights to privacy, as secured by the Fourth and Fifth Amendments.

92 • The income tax provisions have NO legal force or effect inside the 50 States of the Union.

93 • Income tax provisions are forms of perjury, and possibly misprision of perjury by ommission, which are serious federal offenses.

94 • There is ample evidence to indicate that IRS agents bribe U.S. Attorneys, federal judges, and even the Office of the President with huge kickbacks every time a criminal indictment is issued by a federal grand jury against an illegal tax protester.

95 • The IRS is a federal government subcontractor and a Puerto Rico Trust.

96 • The IRS cannot lawfully levy personal property, or bank accounts, without Notice, a Hearing, and due process of law resulting in a valid warrant or court order.

97 • No government services are funded by federal income taxes.

98 • The final report of the Grace Commission, convened under President Ronald Reagan, quietly admitted that none of the funds they collect from federal income taxes goes to pay for any government services.

99 • The availability of correct information about federal government operations is fundamental to maintaining the freedom of the American People.

100 • No statutes create a specific liability for taxes imposed by subtitle A of the IRC.

101 • Americans are being misled to believe that the "Internal Revenue Service" is a United States organization.

102 • The "Internal Revenue Service" is not a United States organization nor is it part of any other country, state, county, or city.

103 • The IRS a private corporation incorporated in Delaware as a for-profit debt collection agency operating under the purview of Title 15 of the "US Code" and the "US Constitution" instead of Title 26 of the "IR Code".

104 • Title 15 of the US Code relates to "Verified Assessment" in that debt collectors are required to provide proof signed under penalty of perjury to validate any debt that debt collectors claim a person owes to the IRS.

105 • Debt collectors can not validate any debt that they claim is owed to the IRS in a documented response signed as a notarized affiant under the penalty of perjury.

106 • The IRS is not a part of the U.S. Government that can mail a letterhead that says: "U.S. Department of the Treasury - Internal Revenue Service".

107 • Liability for the individual income tax applies only to employees and agents of the U.S. Government and to those who manufacture and sell alcohol, tobacco, and fire arms, or other controlled substances.

108 • Liability for the individual income tax applies only to 14th Amendment citizens of the corporate United States and its territories and possessions.

109 • Any document made under Internal Revenue laws and regulations must contain or be verified by a written declaration made under the penalty of perjury according to Section 6065 of the Internal Revenue Code.

110 • The United States was declared bankrupt by President Roosevelt in June of 1933.

111 • The Internal Revenue Department of the United States Treasury is a separate entity from the Internal Revenue Service that is a collection agency of the non-federal Federal Reserve Bank.

112 • All obligations owing to the Internal Revenue Service can be discharged by a sovereign citizen through the United States Treasury per HJR 192 of June 5, 1933 upon one's private personal demand.

113 • The IRS is not registered to do business or perform commercial matters in any state.

114 • People give the IRS money without demanding proof of claim, or even if the IRS is "licenced" to make commercial "offers" of credit based on "arbitrary" estimates.

115 • The IRS never has and never will issue a valid assessment in lien or levy form; such is not possible without affidavits sworn under the penalty of perjury and under commercial liability.

116 • A valid assessment requires a foundational instrument — a contract signed with the debtor's wet-ink autograph showing him in default.

117 • A valid assessment requires a list of the goods and services provided by the IRS, or of damages done.

118 • The fictitious entity called WILLIAM MESSIER is a corporation — as defined in 15 USCA § 44 (U.S. Code Annotated).

119 • F. William Messier's UCC Financing Statement gives public notice that he the lawful man has a claim against the debtor, WILLIAM MESSIER, the unincorporated strawman corporate trust, and all of his assets.

120 • F. William Messier has thereby taken this strawman entity "out of the state"; out of the jurisdiction of a fictitious entity into his private domain; thus the entity became an unincorporated corporate trust "foreign" to the state.

121 • F. William Messier's UCC Financing Statement shows that he has an enforceable security interest in the strawman debtor's property.

122 • F. William Messier's UCC Financing Statement is filed with the Secretary of States, and the Cumberland County registry of deeds, and as such is a public record.

123 • The United States - US - U.S. - USA - America is a federal corporation under Title 28 USC 3002(5) Chapter 176.

124 • The United States is a corporation under 534 Federal Supplement 724.

125 • The United States is a corporation, originally incorporated February 21, 1871 under the name of "District of Columbia" per 16 Stat. 419 Chapter 62.

126 • The United States is a bankrupt organization per House Joint Resolution 192 of June 5, 1933; Senate Report 93-549; and Executive Orders 6072, 6102 and 6246.

127 • The United States is a de facto government; originally the ten square mile tract ceded by Maryland and Virginia comprising Washington, D.C. plus its possessions, territories, arsenals and forts.

128 • The United States, as a corporation, has no more authority to implement its laws against "We the People" than does the Mac Donald Corporation, — except for the contracts we've signed as surety for our strawman with the United States and the foreign Creditor Bankers.

129 • The contracts we've signed as surety for our strawman with the United States and the foreign Creditor Bankers are actually not with us, but with our artificial entity or "person" which appears to be us but is spelled with ALL CAPITAL LETTERS.

130 • The contracts we've signed as surety for our strawman with the United States and the foreign Creditor Bankers were done under Vice-Admiralty Courts established in the Queen's possessions beyond the seas, with jurisdiction over Maritime causes, including those relating to prize.

131 • The United States of America is lawfully the possession of the English Crown per original commercial joint venture agreement between the colonies and the Crown and the Constitution which brought all the states (only) back under British ownership and rule.

132 • The sovereign American people, however, had sovereign standing in law, independent of any connection to the states or the Crown.

133 • The sovereignty of the American people necessitated that the people be brought back, one at a time, under British Rule, and the Commercial process was the method of choice in order to accomplish this recapturing task.

134 • This recapturing task was accomplished first through the 14th Amendment and then through the registration of our birth certificate and private property.

135 • All courts in America are Vice-Admiralty courts in the Crown's private commerce in this United States; the Queen's possession beyond the sea.

The Foregoing claims stand as truth under the Commercial law of the Uniform Commercial Code (UCC) unless rebutted point for point under the penalty of perjury by the Accused parties.

The Accused failed to document their positions and authority by NOT providing the following documents:

(1) the statutes that impose upon F. William Messier an obligation to provide any private personal papers to them.

(2) specific copies of their delegation orders from the Secretary down to the Commissioner, down to the District Director, and down to them.

(3) copies of any notices sent to F. William Messier that informed him that he is required to keep records and papers for the Secretary or the IRS or them; and produce such.

(4) copies of any determinations or decisions that show that F. William Messier is liable to the United States of America corporation or the IRS for any taxes.

(5) copies of any documents or decisions that show how F. William Messier came within the taxing authority of the corporate United States of America.

(6) Validation of any debt that the Accused claim F. William Messier owes to the IRS in a documented response signed as a notarized affiant under the penalty of perjury as is required by law.

(7) proof that the Accused are part of the U.S. Government and a letterhead that says U.S. Department of the Treasury - Internal Revenue Service if they are part of the U.S. Government.

(8) all documents on which the Accused base their claim that F. William Messier has any obligation to the Accused or their Service or the corporate United States and that F. William Messier is required to produce books and records for their examination.

(9) copies of all documents that identify how F. William Messier came within the purview of the statutes which they claim obligate him to produce personal documents for their examination.

(10) all documents of determination that indicate F. William Messier is liable or subject to any statute that they or their Service claim to have authority to enforce.

(11) copies of all documents that identify the facts on which those determinations were made.

(12) copies of all statutes on which those facts were applied to make any of the determinations that F. William Messier is liable or subject.

(13) copies of the Notices sent or served upon F. William Messier prior to making those determinations.

(14) copies of their delegation of authority to inquire into F. William Messier's personal affairs or make any demand upon him or his customers, and the delegations of authority of those who made the above determinations that F. William Messier is liable or subject to those determinations.

(15) copies of the Accused's document of appointment to the position which they now hold and copies of the documents that identify by name title, position, G.S.#, and office, each party who participated in any aspect of the above determinations.

(16) the document that describes the procedural format for expungement of alleged determinations, improperly or unlawfully made within and by their Service.

Without this specific documentation of authority F. William Messier presumes that none exists.

F. William Messier is in receipt of many form letter type NOTICES OF LEVY from the agency that the Accused serve, that carry a stamped signature (or no signature at all) which claims that an IRS agent has been assigned to examine alleged federal tax returns of his.

The Accused are in error and proceeding on false assumptions if they believe that F. William Messier has some obligation of tax liability to them or the Internal Revenue Service, debt collection agency of the non-federal Federal Reserve Bank.

F. William Messier gave teach of the Accused NOTICE of those errors and he declared his objection to any such presumed claims by them or anyone else in their Internal Revenue Service. F. William Messier denies that he has any obligation of tax liability to the Accused or to the IRS.

It is F. William Messier's intention to obey all laws that legitimately impose a requirement or obligation upon him. However, he has no desire to volunteer where no obligation exists, especially when the waiver of his rights is involved. He is relying on what the Supreme Court held long ago:

> "An individual may be under no obligation to do a particular thing, and his failure to act creates no liability; but if he voluntarily attempts to act and do a particular thing, he comes under an implied obligation in respect to the manner in which he does it." Guardian T&D Co. v. Fisher (1906) 26 S.Ct. 186,188.

Therefore, F. William Messier has determined that he is not one of the Accused's subjects. Neither is he one to whom they can demand that he produce personal documents and records for their review or that he has any obligation to submit those records for an examination by them or others for any purpose.

What's more, F. William Messier has determined that the designation "1040" for the type of tax shown on the IRS' Notices of Federal Tax Liens that the IRS claims he is liable for does not pertain to Form 1040; but misleadingly refers to Section 1040 of the tax code under Subtitle B which pertains to profit and gain on the Transfer by the executor of an estate of certain real property imposed upon the executor under Section 1040 of the tax code which is an estate tax that has nothing to do with

Subtitle A of the tax code referring to income taxes.

In regard to the Accused's false accusations regarding 26 USC Sect. 7212 - Attempt to interfere with administration of internal revenue laws:

Re: Sect. 7212(a) Corrupt or forcible interference, an honest request for discovery cannot be taken as Corrupt or forcible interference.

Re: Sect. 7212(b) Forcible rescue of seized property, no property has been forcibly rescued or seized.

Furthermore, Congress never enacted Title 26 as positive Law and Title 26 is irrelevant to action taken under Title 15 of the Fair Debt Collections Practices Act which pertains to F. William Messier's defense and the IRS.

> 26 USC § 7212 - Attempts to interfere with administration of internal revenue laws
>
> (a) Corrupt or forcible interference
>
> Whoever corruptly or by force or threats of force (including any threatening letter or communication) endeavors to intimidate or impede any officer or employee of the United States acting in an official capacity under this title, or in any other way corruptly or by force or threats of force (including any threatening letter or communication) obstructs or impedes, or endeavors to obstruct or impede, the due administration of this title, shall, upon conviction thereof, be fined not more than $5,000, or imprisoned not more than 3 years, or both, except that if the offense is committed only by threats of force, the person convicted thereof shall be fined not more than $3,000, or imprisoned not more than 1 year, or both. The term "threats of force", as used in this subsection, means threats of bodily harm to the officer or employee of the United States or to a member of his family.
>
> (b) Forcible rescue of seized property
>
> Any person who forcibly rescues or causes to be rescued any property after it shall have been seized under this title, or shall attempt or endeavor so to do, shall, excepting in cases otherwise provided for, for every such offense, be fined not more than $500, or not more than double the value of the property so rescued, whichever is the greater, or be imprisoned not more than 2 years.

F. William Messier's authority for making his demand for verification of the Accused's authority has been well established as follows:

> "Whatever the form in which the Government functions, anyone entering into an arrangement with the Government takes the risk of having accurately ascertained that he who purports to act for the Government stays within the bounds of his authority... and this is so even though, as here, the agent himself may have been unaware of the limitations upon his authority." — Federal Crop Insurance Corporation v. Merrill, 332 U.S. 380 at 384 (1947).

F. William Messier stands on the basis of Title 15 U.S.C. Sections 1692-1692p — and reserved his human rights.

Section 805(b) COMMUNICATION WITH THIRD PARTIES: "without the prior consent of the consumer a debt collector may not communicate with any person other than a consumer, etc."

Section 807(1) False or misleading representations: "A debt collector may not use any false, deceptive or mis-leading representation or means in connection with the collection of any debt."

(1) "The false implication that the debt collector is affiliated with the United States..."

(2) "The false representation of (A) the character of any debt..."

F. William Messier offered to settle this matter out of court by the Accused ceasing collection activities and returning his funds without further penalty to them personally and the Accused failed to respond to his offer by correcting their faults by the prompt return of his funds in lieu of the documents requested above.

F. William Messier did not hear from the Accused within the time period offered so their lack of response established the presumption that they do not have the documentation or the authority to support their claim to any requirement or obligation upon F. William Messier which failure constitutes a breach of contract.

TIMELY NOTICE AND DEMAND HAS BEEN GIVEN THEM (18 U.S.C.S. 4, 2382)

Testified by F. William Messier AND David Everett Robinson on the 3rd day of August, in the year of our Lord 2012 under the penalty of perjury.

Attached:
Copies of Maine Republic Email Alerts
　　#171 The IRS - The Biggest Lie
　　#174 The Organic Act of 1871
　　#166 Layers of Conspiracy
　　#087 The Internal Revenue is not the Internal Revenue Service
　　#088 Nil-dicit Judgment ("he says nothing" judgment)
　　#090 IRS Levis and Liens
　　#094 IRS Strategy
　　#095 Internal Revenue Service Personnel
　　#156 Maine Governor Paul LePage Speaks Out!!!
　　#157 Request for Discovery

AFFIDVIT OF FOREIGN STATUS

PREAMBLE

The following **Affidavit of Foreign Status** is a public notice to all interested parties concerning the Affiant's "birthrights" and his "status" as an "AMERICAN INHABITANT", as that status would apply with respect to the American States (the 50 independent States of the Union) and also with respect to the "United States", as follows:

1 • The Affiant, **F. William Messier**, was naturally born as a free Sovereign in Maine, which is one of the sovereign States of the Union of several States joined together to comprise the Confederation known as the United States of America.

2 • The Affiant is, therefore, a "non-resident alien" individual with respect to the United States, which entity obtains its exclusive legislative authority and jurisdiction from Article 1, Section 8, Clause 17 and Article 4, Section 3, Clause 2 of the Constitution <u>for</u> the United States of America.

3 • The Affiant's parents were sovereigns also; born in sovereign States of the Union.

4 • As the progeny of Sovereign people, the Affiant was born "...one of the sovergin people... A constituent member of the sovereignty synonymous with the people." *Scott v. Sanford*, 19 How. 404.

5 • The Affiant is alien to a so-called "14th Amendment United States citizen", and also nonresident to so-called "14th Amendment State residency", and therefore, he is a "nonresident alien" with respect to both.

6 • As a sovereign whose Citizenship originated in Maine by birth, and who has remained intact in Maine since then, the Affiant is also a foreigner (alien) with respect to the other 49 States of the Union and with respect to the "United States."

7 • As a consequence of his birth the Affiant is an "American Inhabitant."

8 • The Affiant, to the best of his knowledge and belief, has not entered into any valid agreements of "voluntary servitude".

9 • The Affiant is a "NONRESIDENT ALIEN" with respect to the "United States" as that term is defined and used within the Internal Revenue Code (IRC) (Title 26, United States Code) and/or Title 27 and the rules and regulations promulgated thereunder as follows:

The Internal Revenue Code (Title 26, United States Code) and associated federal regulations, clearly and thoroughly make provision for Americans born and living within one of the 50 Sovereign States of America, to wit:

Section 1.871-4 Proof of residence of aliens.

(a)   **Rules of evidence.** The following rules of evidence shall govern in determining whether or not an alien within the United States has acquired residence therein for purposes of the income tax.

(b)   **Nonresidence presumed.** An alien by reason of his alienage is presumed to be a non resident alien.   [26 CFR 1.871-4]

10 • The Affiant was not born or naturalized in the "United states", consequently he is not a "citizen of the United States" nor a "United States citizen", as those terms are defined and used within the Internal Revenue Code (26 USC) and/or Title 27 and the rules and regulations promulgated thereunder, and therefore he is not subject to the limited, exclusive territorial or political jurisdiction and authority of the "United States" as defined.

The "United States" is definitive and specific when it defines one of its citizens, as follows:

Section 1.1-1

(c)   **Who is a citizen.** Every person born or naturalized in the United States and subject to its jurisdiction is a citizen.   [26 CFR 1.1-1(c)]

11 • The Affiant is not a "citizen of the United States" nor a "United States citizen living abroad", as those phrases are defined and used in the Internal Revenue Code (26 USC) and/or Title 27 and the rules and regulations promulgated thereunder.

12 • The Affiant is not a "resident alien residing within the geographical boundaries of the United States", as that phrase is defined and used in the Internal Revenue Code (26 USC) and/or Title 27 and the rules and regulations promulgated thereunder.

13 • The Affiant is not a "United States person", a "domestic corporation", "estate", "trust", "fiduciary", or "partnership" as those terms are defined and used in the Internal Revenue Code (26 USC) and/or Title 27 and the rules and regulations promulgated thereunder.

14 • The Affiant is not an "Officer", "employee", or "elected official" of the "United States" or a "State" or of any political subdivision thereof, nor of the District of Columbia, nor of any agency or instrumentality of one or more of the foregoing, nor an "officer" of a "United States corporation", as those terms are defined and used in the Internal Revenue Code (26 USC) and/or Title 27 and the rules and regulations promulgated thereunder.

15 • The Affiant receives no "income with respect to employment" from any sources within the territorial jurisdiction of the "United States" and does not have an "office or other fixed place of business" within the "United States" from which the Affiant derives any "income" or "wages" as such, as those terms and phrases are used and defined within the Internal Revenue Code (26 IRC) and/or Title 27 and the rules and regulations promulgated thereunder.

16 • The Affiant has never engaged in the conduct of a "trade" or "business" within the "united States", nor does the Affiant receive any income or other remuneration effectively connected with the conduct of a "trade" or "business" within the "United States", as those terms are defined and used in the Internal Revenue Code (26 USC) and/or Title 27 and the rules and regulations promulgated thereunder.

17 • The Affiant receives no "income", "wages", "self-employment income" or "other remuneration" from sources within the "United States", as those terms are defined and used and defined within the Internal Revenue Code (26 IRC) and/or Title 27 and the rules and regulations promulgated thereunder.

18 • All remuneration paid to the Affiant is for services rendered outside (without) the exclusive territorial, political and legislative jurisdiction and authority of the "united States".

19 • The Affiant has never had an "office" or "place of business" within the "United States", as those terms are defined and used and defined within the Internal Revenue Code (26 IRC) and/or Title 27 and the rules and regulations promulgated thereunder.

20 • The Affiant has never been a "United States employer", nor "employer", nor "employee" which also includes but is not limited to an "employee" and/or "employer" for a "United States" "household", and/or "agricultural" activity, as those terms are defined and used and defined within the Internal Revenue Code (26 IRC) and/or Title 27 and the rules and regulations promulgated thereunder.

21 • The Affiant has never been involved in any "commerce" within the territorial jurisdiction of the "United States" which also includes but is not limited to "alcohol", "tobacco" and "firearms" and Title 16, Subtitle D and E excises and privileged occupations, as those are defined and used and defined within the Internal Revenue Code (26 IRC) and/or Title 27 and the rules and regulations promulgated thereunder.

22 • The Affiant has never been a "United States" "withholding agent" as those are defined and used and defined within the Internal Revenue Code (26 IRC) and/or Title 27 and the rules and regulations promulgated thereunder.

23 • The Affiant has no liability for any type, kind or class of Federal Income Tax in past years, and was and is entitled to a full and complete refund of any amounts withheld, because any liability asserted and amounts withheld were premised upon a mutual mistake or facts regarding the Affiant's status.

24 • The Affiant has never knowingly, intentionally, and voluntarily changed his Citizenship status nor has he ever knowingly, intentionally, and voluntarily elected to be treated as a "resident" of the "United States".

25 • The Affiant, to the best of his current knowledge, owes no "tax" of any type, class or kind to the "United States" as those are defined and used and defined within the Internal Revenue Code (26 IRC) and/or Title 27 and the rules and regulations promulgated thereunder.

26 • The Affiant anticipates no liability for any type, class or kind of federal income tax in the current year, because the Affiant does not intend to reside in the "United States", he does not intend to be treated as either a "resident" or a "citizen" of the "United States", he is not and does not intend to be involved in the conduct of any "trade" or "business" within the "United States", as those are defined and used and defined within the Internal Revenue Code (26 IRC) and/or Title 27 and the rules and regulations promulgated thereunder.

27 • The Affiant, by means or knowingly intelligent acts done with sufficient awareness of the relevant circumstances and consequences (*Brady v. US*, 397 US 742, 748 (1970)) never agreed or consented to be given a federal Social Security Number (SSN)), same said as to a federal Employee Identification Number (EIN) and therefore waives and releases from liability the "United States" and any State of the Union of 50 States, for any present or future benefits that the Affiant may be entitled to claim under the Old-Age Survivors and the Disability Insurance Act and/or the Federal Unemployment Tax Act.

28 • The Affiant makes to claim to any present of future benefits under any of the foregoing.

29 • I, **F. William Messier**, am a natural born free inhabitant, and as such, a Sovereign Citizen/Principal inhabiting the Maine Republic.

30 • I, **F. William Messier**, am not "within the United States" but lawfully am "without the United States" (per Title 28, USC, Section 1746, Subsection 1), and therefore have no standing capacity to sign any tax form which displays the perjury clause pursuant to Title 28, Section 1746, Subsection 2.

PLEASE NOTE WELL: At no time will the Affiant construe any of the foregoing terms defined within the Internal Revenue Code, Title 26, United States Code, or within any of the other United State Codes, in a metaphorical sense. When terms are not words of art and are explicitly defined within the Code and/or within a Statute, the Affiant relies at all times upon the clear language of the terms as they are defined therein, **NO MORE** and **NO LESS.**

> ... When aid to construction of the meaning of words, as used in the statute, is available, there certainly can be no "rule of law" which forbids its use however clear the words may appear on "superficial examination". [*United States v. American Trucking Association*] [310 US 534, 543, 544 (1939)]

This sworn certification is being executed WITHOUT the "United States".

I affirm under penalty of perjury, under the laws of the United States of America, that I executed the foregoing for the purposes and considerations herein expressed, in the capacity stated, and that the statements contained here are true and correct to the best of my knowledge and belief.

F. William Messier, Citizen/Principal, by special Appearance, in Propria Persona (*in my own person*) proceeding Sui Juris (*of full age and capacity, possessing full social and civil rights*).

Complaint and Motion for Summary Judgement or Jury Trial

AFFIRMATION

I, <u>David Everett Robinson</u>, *do hereby affirm that the foregoing information provided by me is true and correct to the best of my knowledge and belief. I understand that any false, misleading, or untrue statements, accusations or allegations made by me, either orally or in writing to any person (s) investigating this complaint may subject me to civil and/or criminal prosecution.*

I realize that it may become necessary during the investigation of this complaint for me to meet with representatives of the Cumberland County sheriff's Office to discuss this complaint, either in the presence or absence of the accused party (s) at the discretion of the department. I hereby accept the premise that if any action is initiated through a court or administrative proceeding as a result of my complaint, my testimony before these hearings may be required. I agree to make myself available as a witness before either of the aforesaid bodies, upon request by the sheriff or his/her designee.

Signed, <u>David Everett Robinson</u> *this* <u>4th</u> *day of* <u>August</u> *2012 in*

the Town/City of <u>Brunswick</u> *, State of Maine.*

The Internal Revenue is not the Internal Revenue Service

The **Internal Revenue** of the United States government, is not the **Internal Revenue Service** of the Federal Reserve Bank.

The **Internal Revenue** determines tax debts for the United States, while the **Internal Revenue Service** collects those tax debts for the Federal Reserve Bank.

It's all about the "bill" and not the "law".

Use Title 15 for your defense, instead of Title 26 and the Constitution. Title 15 relates to "verified Assessment". The collector must provide **proof of the debt** to validate the debt. Any case involving debt must be held in a judicial district court.

The IRS circumvents the Constitution by using **their** tax law *(Title 26)* to confuse their victims.

Tax law doesn't apply. The IRS is a **debt collection agency** of the non-federal Federal Reserve Bank. Thus, the IRS is required to follow Title 15 of the United States Code.

What's more, the IRS has no way to verify the debt — unless you voluntarily assess *yourself* for an "income" debt that you do not owe.

The IRS, by its corporate charter and its own admission, is a debt collection agency. Debt collection agencies are subject to Title 15 of the United States Code — not to USC Title 26.

It seems that the primary strategy of the IRS is to get us to fight the wrong battle — to play the wrong game in the wrong court.

Although Title 26 is the Internal Revenue Code— the Code of the Internal Revenue, — the IRS is a collection agency of the Federal Reserve Bank and collection agencies must follow Title 15.

If you don't demand that the IRS verify the debt, then you are agreeing that the IRS' "bill" is valid. In other words, you are voluntarily condemning yourself to an "income" tax that you do not otherwise owe.

This is no different that a court officer tricking you into fighting an *accusation,* when you should be fighting the *charge.*

So what is the Remedy for this case?

Title 15 > Chapter 41 > Subchapter V > **Section 1692**

§ 1692. Congressional findings and declaration of purpose.

(a) Abusive practices

[*The invasion of individual privacy is an abusive, deceptive, and unfair debt collection practice.*]

(e) Purposes

[*It is the purpose of this subchapter...to protect consumers against debt collection abuses.*]

§ 1692a. Definitions

(5) [*The term "debt" means any obligation...whether or not such obliga-tion has been reduced to judgment.*]

§ 1692b. Acquisition of location information. Any debt collector...shall

(1) The false representation or implication that the debt collector is vouched for, bonded by, or affiliated with the United States or any State, including the use of any badge, uniform, or facsimile thereof.

HERE'S THE SILVER BULLET

Title 26 USC has nothing to do with the INTERNAL REVENUE SERVICE, it only applies to the INTERNAL REVENUE.

The giveaway is in Title 26, section 7802(b)(1)(c)

7802 INTERNAL REVENUE SERVICE OVERSIGHT BOARD

(b)(1)(c) one member shall be the Commissioner of the Internal Revenue.

Hence, "The Internal Revenue Code" is not "The Internal Revenue Service Code".

The "Internal Revenue" and the Internal Revenue Service" are two separate and distinct entities.

The "Internal Revenue" is a govern-ment agency under the scope of Title 26.

The "Internal Revenue Service" us a private for profit corporation under the scope of Title 15.

If you look up Internal Revenue Service in the Index of Title 26 you will discover that it is only mentioned in a few sections. None of which have anything to do with determining the tax, they only deal with governance, collection and the like.

UNDISPUTED CONCLUSIONS

Title 15 > Chapter 41 > Sub-chapter V > Section 1692 is and act of Congress designed to protect *natural persons*.

1692a. The term *"consumer"* means any *natural person* obligated or allegedly obligated to pay any debt.

THE INTERNAL REVENUE SERVICE is not part of the United States Government. See: *Diversified Metal Products v. T-Bow Co. Trust/ IRS 93-405-E-EJL.*

THE INTERNAL REVENUE SERVICE is incorporated in Delaware **as a collection agency for a Puerto Rico company; INTERNAL REVENUE TAX AND AUDIT SERVICE (IRS)** For Profit General Delaware Corporation. Incorporation Date 7/12/33, File No. 0325720.

Several Corporations involved with the INTERNAL REVENUE SERVICE are also unlawfully acting under color of law as government agencies, as well.

Consider adding the word "Service" to other entities and see how it works.

FEDERAL RESERVE ASSOCIA-TION (Federal Reserve) Non-profit Delaware Corporation. Incorporation Date 9/13/14 File No. 0042817

CENTRAL INTELLIGENCE AUTHORITY INC. (CIA) Non-profit Delaware Corporation. Incorporation Date 3/9/83 File No. 2004409

UNITED STATES OF AMERICA, INC. Non-profit Delaware Corporation. Incorporation Date 4/19/89 File No. 2193946

FEDERAL LAND ACQUISITION CORP. For-profit Delaware Corporation. Incorporation Date 8/22/80. File No. 0897960

RTC COMMERCIAL ASSETS TRUST 1995-NP3-2. For-profit Delaware Corporation. Incorporation Date 10/24/95. File No. 2554768

SOCIAL SECURITY CORP., DEPT. OF HEALTH, EDUCATION AND WELFARE. For-profit Delaware Statutory Trust. Incorporation Date 11/13/89. File No. 2213135

"ad Christi potentium et gloriam"
(for the power and glory of Christ)

Maine Republic *Email Alert*

No.088

"*. . . that I should bear witness unto the truth.*" — *John 18:33* // *David E. Robinson, Publisher*

"*. . . if the trumpet give an uncertain sound, who shall prepare himself for battle?*" — *I Corinthians 14:8* — 05/04/12

Nil-Dicit Judgment (*"he says nothing" judgment*)

The first rule of winning in court is to win before going to court. **The second rule** is to make the other party argue about something other than the case. IRS attorneys know this, so we should know this too.

The IRS is a debt collection service.

When the IRS charges someone with willful failure to file under civil law they are actually *billing the victim* for a tax. The victim then tries to fight the IRS using the Constitution and/or Title 26 of the United States Code without ever asking for a *verified assessment* of the debt under Title 15.

This *lack of request* gives the IRS the ability to obtain a *nil-dicit judgment* against the victim in UNITED STATES DISTRICT COURT, making the bill a lawful bill.

Once the bill is deemed lawful, the IRS gets to claim that the victim is fraudulently refusing to pay a legal debt, and converts the refusal to pay into some kind of criminal act.

Whereas in reality, since the IRS is a debt collection service for the non-federal Federal Reserve Bank, the victim can require that the IRS verify the assessment, *which the IRS cannot do,* — and if it could, the victim could make the IRS take the action to the jurisdictional district the alleged debtor is in.

However the IRS cannot verify the alleged debt assessment; only the victim can do that by admitting the claim.

Going to court and arguing about taxes using Title 26 is ineffective for the following reasons:

1. Title 26 is used by the government to *determine* the tax.

2. The IRS is a debt collection service, not a government agency. *see Diversified Metal v. T-Bow Trust/IRS*

3. The bill issued by the U.S. Treasury *(under Title 26)* becomes a debt collectable by the IRS *(which has to follow Title 15).*

4. If you fight the IRS under Title 26, you are fighting something they have nothing to do with. It's like contesting the electric bill to the mail man, he will just think you are a nag, and he can't do anything about it anyhow.

5. The bill has already been adjudicated under *nil-dicit judgment* and stands *if not contested under Title 15. You cannot contest the bill under Title 26 since that is the government code on how to figure the bill, not the bill itself.*

6. Demanding that the IRS verify the assessment *(the bill)* requires them to cease and desist *(under Title 15)* until they supply the documents.

7. The IRS cannot supply the requisite documents and therefore you have beat them before going to court. *see Rule 1.*

8. If you go to court you can argue the correct issue, *the bill,* not how they *determined* the bill, thusly you can win by arguing the right argument. *rule 2.*

9. You can force the IRS to do the action in the judicial district, *i.e. the court nearest the debtor,* which they will not do, and therefore you won't go to court. *see YHWH's scriptures.*

Title 26 > *Subtitle F* > *Chapter 76* > *Subchapter A* > *Section 7408*

§ 7408. *Actions to enjoin specified conduct related to tax shelters and reportable transactions.*

(d) Citizens and residents outside the United States

If any citizen or resident of the United States does not reside in, and does not have his principal place of business in, any United States judicial district, such citizen or resident shall be treated for purposes of this section as residing in the District of Columbia.

One of the common denominators of acquittals is that somewhere or somehow the victim did some type of request for assessment that was never affirmed.

This is diametrically opposite to all the victims who lost using Title 26 and the absence of applicability to the code.

In summary, just like a charge in a traffic ticket, don't fight the law and *their* reasoning, deny the bill and require them to prove that the bill exists as a matter of record, before they *make* it a matter of record under *nil-dicit judgment* because you didn't deny it.

Example:

A contractor (government under Title 26) issues you (contractee) a bill through their third party collection service (IRS), you do not respond. Third party collector service, whose actions and remedies are defined in Title 15, goes to court ex-parte and receives a nil-dicit judgment. You get dragged into a foreign court (USDC) and attempt to fight the contractor and their rules for issuing the bill under the Constitution and/or Title 26, neither of which applies, since it is the bill being discussed, not the entity that issued the bill or how said entity determined the amount. Any attorney would tell you that this is a waste of time. You (contractee) must first void the bill under the appropriate code (Title 15) and demand the case be kept in the proper jurisdiction (the nearest judicial district).

In essence, Title 26 applies to the government entity that determined the bill and Title 15 applies to the collection agency attacking you for payment.

Title 26, THE IRC has little to do with the IRS.

IRS Levys and Liens

Written By - Rico S. Giron, Future Sheriff of San Miguel County, New Mexico. http://ricoforsheriff.com

The Federal Reserve Bank, a.k.a. the IRS, is the biggest lie and scam in world history.

I.R.S. - are the three most frightening and loathed letters in the English language.

This deep-seated fear and loathing serves a very specific purpose. It serves to keep the People of America enslaved in submission to an illusion, a lie. It is an emotional and psychological chain around the neck of the American people.

The IRS has a horrible reputation and has earned every bit of it, it has by their own admissions committed crimes against innocent Citizens, and continues to be the **"Gestapo" of America** today.

They confiscate more homes, destroy more families, take more money, ruin more lives, and commit more crimes than all the street gangs combined.

They are indeed vivid proof that *"The greatest threat we face as a nation is our own Federal Government!"* — from "The County Sheriff: America's Last Hope", by author Richard Mack.

Here it is in a nutshell:

The IRS is a private, debt collection agency for the private banking system known as the Federal Reserve Bank.

The IRS is not a government agency. I repeat, the IRS is not a government agency. Never has been, never will be.

The IRS is formerly the Bureau of Internal Revenue (BIR) situated in, and with authority only in, the Philippine Islands (Trust Fund # 61); moved into Puerto Rico (Trust Fund # 62).

In the 1950's, with the stroke of the pen, the BIR was transformed into the current, notorious IRS and brought onto the 50 united States.

This was done without any Congressional authority whatsoever. There is no Congressional authority for the IRS to exist and operate in the 50 states of the Union recorded anywhere in any law-books.

Again, keep in mind, that the IRS is the **"Private, debt collection agency for the private banking system known as the Federal Reserve Bank(s)".**

Due to the naive ignorance of the American people, most Americans do not realize that there are two titles 26.

Title 26, Internal Revenue Code, is the "Debt Collection Manual" for the IRS.

This manual has nothing with Constitutional Rights. The IRS does not collect an "income tax". The IRS is simply collecting a "user fee" payable to the Federal Reserve Bank because we Americans are using a *private credit system.* The user fee had to be disguised as an "income tax" to fool the American people and keep them enslaved.

Title 26, United States Code, is "non-positive" law, which means that no "American Citizen" is subject to it. However, all "U.S. citizens" *are* subject to it. In order to understand "U.S. citizen" you must go to 28 USC, section 3002.

Most "American Citizens" have perhaps *unknowingly,* but *voluntarily,* surrendered their Sovereignty in exchange for the "immunities and privileges" of the 14th Amendment.

There are literally hundreds of unilateral, silent contracts by which American Citizens *declare themselves* to be "U.S. citizens" and thus subject to *both* Titles 26.

By *voluntarily* becoming a "U.S. citizen", every "American Citizen" declares him/herself to be an "indentured servant" (a slave) to the non-federal, Federal Reserve Banking system with no Constitutional Rights whatsoever.

So then, Title 26, USC, is a *private law* that applies only to "U.S. corporate 'citizens'", who are **all** employees of the corporate entity identified at 28 USC, section 3002(15)(A)(B)(C).

(15) "United States" means—

(A) a Federal corporation;

(B) an agency, department, com-mission, board, or other entity of the United States; or

(C) an instrumentality of the United States.

Consider this fact.

When an IRS agent wants to seize property from a Citizen in a County, they must first contact the Sheriff of the County and request assistance in the seizure because the IRS agent has no authority to seize any property at all.

So the IRS agent bamboozles the Sheriff into committing the crime, **for the IRS.**

When the Sheriff seizes property from a Citizen under the *non-authority* of the IRS agent, the Sheriff has committed a Second Degree Felony, **Conversion of Property.**

A second degree felony is incredibly serious!

However, both the IRS agent and the Sheriff, knowingly or unknowingly, count on the ignorance of the Citizen who has no idea what their Lawful Rights are.

Bear this point in mind: If the IRS agent has no authority to seize any property at all, then they cannot *delegate,* or *confer* to the Sheriff what they themselves do not have.

In addition, the Sheriff has no idea that he has engaged in a serious crime.

Here is where the maxim, **"Ignorance of the law is no excuse** *[for violating the law]"* applies. Hence the maxim, **"The Law leaves the wrong-doer where it finds him".**

We do not have an excuse based on

"ad Christi potentium et gloriam"
(for the power and glory of Christ)

Complaint and Motion for Summary Judgement or Jury Trial

IRS Strategy

The IRS operates a clearly defined and very clever scam. Here is how it works.

(1) The IRS presumes a fictional, fraudulent, nebulous, libelous and imaginary assessment against a citizen.

(2) The IRS presents this assessment as a Notice of Tax Lien to the County Recorder.

(3) A Notice of Tax Lien is supposed to instruct the tax "debtor" as to where the actual Tax Lien can be found, studied, and copied so that it can be challenged if necessary, but the Notice of Tax Lien never does provide that information because the IRS never produces any Tax Liens to which a Notice could refer.

(4) An unlawful statute injected into the Revised Code of Washington at RCW 60.68.045 by the IRS, and uncritically allowed to reside there by legislators, other officers of the government, and citizens, directs the County Recorder to enter the "Notice of Tax Lien" on a "Tax Lien" Index.

(5) But a "Notice of Tax Lien" does not contain a sworn (affidavit) assessment and is therefore only a non-negotiable/non-"spendable" paper instrument, which means that it cannot be used as money after maturing unchallenged 90 days, to procure, seize and sell property.

(6) And a Lien, any lien, if lawfully constructed must contain a sworn (affidavit) assessment as part of the full disclosure requirement of all negotiable instruments, and is therefore a negotiable/"spendable" paper instrument, which means that it can be used as money after maturing unchallenged for 90 days, to procure, seize and sell property.

(7) Since the IRS never presents a Tax Lien to the County Recorder, because IRS agents do not want the liability for presenting a false, fraudulent, nebulous, and/or libelous assessment, it must procure *or suborn* the County Recorder to do IRS counterfeiting for it by counterfeiting the *appearance* of the existence of a Tax Lien by *changing* the title from a Notice into a Lien by unlawfully entering it on the wrong Index, a Tax Lien Index.

(8) By changing the title from a Notice into a Lien, the County Recorder has converted a non-negotiable/non-"spendable" paper into a negotiable/"spendable" ledger entry, and has therefore *counterfeited a currency,* for the IRS, lacking full disclosure.

(9) Then, all the IRS has to do is to ask the County Recorder for a Certified Copy of the **Tax Lien Index** to "prove" that a Lien has been filed. This Certified Copy of the **Tax Lien Index** has the same power in commerce as a Federal Reserve Note because it can be used as money to procure, seize and sell property, to transfer property from the citizens to the IRS.

(10) Once the IRS has the Certified Copy of the **Tax Lien Index** implying the filing of a Lien, the IRS can begin taking wages, bank accounts, investments, social security payments, retirement benefits, houses, cars, and just about anything else that will bring cash to the IRS directly or by auction.

(11) The Public, the Legal Establishment, and the Courts, are all conditioned by threats of IRS retaliation to do whatever the IRS dictates, so the scam is complete. Therefore, there is no remedy through the judicial courts.

The ONLY REMEDY of this problem is to ignore the judicial system and to use the same ancient and timeless system of commerce which the IRS uses, but to use the commercial system lawfully and properly by doing everything with **sworn affidavits containing full disclosure** (Exodus 20:16).

"ad Christi potentium et gloriam"
(for the power and glory of Christ)

Maine Republic *Email Alert*

No.095

". . . that I should bear witness unto the truth." — John 18:33 // David E. Robinson, Publisher

". . . if the trumpet give an uncertain sound, who shall prepare himself for battle?" — I Corinthians 14:8 — 05/12/12

Internal Revenue Service Personnel

Internal Revenue Service Personnel have no authority whatever to levy salaries and wages from privately owned companies.

IRS authority is applicable solely to **government agencies and personnel** by 26 U.S.C. 6331(a): "Levy may be made upon the accrued salary or wages of any officer, employee, or elected official, of the United States, the District of Columbia, or any agency or instrumentality of the United States or the District of Columbia, by serving a **notice of levy on the employer.**"

First, such notices must include a **Form 668B**, which is the actual levy.

Second, only those large businesses and governmental units that have designated officers and written agreements are authorized to receive notices of levy by mail.

Third, to complete the levy, another form, **Form 668C**, must be served, but cannot be served by mail; it must be served in person. That completes **service of "notice of levy".**

Absent **Form 668B** there is no evidence that there is a levy. In the event the IRS fails to serve **either or both the levy and Form 668C**, service of process is incomplete and the IRS defaults.

In brief, **there can be no seizure before a judgment in a state court is rendered.**

Further, the AGO (Attorney General's Office) states clearly that there are **two forms of judicial process** referred to above, **writs of attachment** and **writs of garnishment**.

Since **a notice of levy is neither,** it should be obvious that it is not **"service of process"** in any legal sense whatsoever. **Federal law says that a levy is served with a writ of attachment.** Writs of attachment have a different purpose than writs of garnishment.

A levy is not a garnishment; a levy is an <u>attachment</u>.

It takes a court action to compel anyone to surrender a consumer's property to another (such as the IRS) without the consumer's consent and over the consumers objection.

In sum, a "<u>notice of levy</u>" is not a levy nor a garnishment.

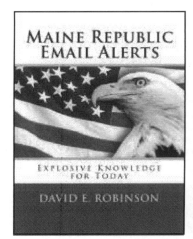

Maine Republic Email Alert

No.171

". . . that I should bear witness unto the truth." — John 18:33 // David E. Robinson, Publisher

". . . if the trumpet give an uncertain sound, who shall prepare himself for battle?" — I Corinthians 14:8 —   07/18/12

The IRS - The Biggest Lie

Posted by F. William Messier, of Brunswick, Maine:

THIS WAS WRITTEN BY A CANDIDATE FOR SHERIFF'S OFFICE IN SAN MATEO COUNTY, CALIFORNIA

IRS Liens and Levies

IRS-The biggest worst deal in World History

IRS-probably the three most frightening letters in the English language. This deep-seated fear and loathing serves a very specific purpose. It serves to keep the People of America in submission to an illusion, a lie.

The IRS has a horrible reputation and has earned every bit of it, has by their own admissions committed crimes against innocent Citizens, and continues today to be the "Gestapo" of America.

They confiscate more homes, destroy more families, take more money, ruin more lives, and commit more crimes than all the street gangs in America combined.

They are indeed vivid proof that the greatest threat we face, as a nation, is our own Federal" Government." [The County Sheriff: America's Last Hope. Author Richard Mack].

Here it is in a nutshell. **The IRS is the "Private, debt collection agency for the private banking system known as the non-federal Federal Reserve Bank".** The IRS is not a government agency. I repeat, the IRS is not a government agency. Never has been, never will be.

The IRS is formerly the Bureau of Internal Revenue (BIR) situated in and with authority only in the Philippine Islands (Trust Fund # 61), and moved into Puerto Rico (Trust Fund # 62).

In the 1950's, with the stroke of a pen, the BIR was transformed into the current notorious IRS and brought onto the 50 united States. This was done without any Congressional authority whatsoever.

There is no Congressional authority for the IRS to exist and operate in the 50 states; recorded anywhere in any law-books. Again, keep in mind, that **the IRS is the "Private, debt collection agency for the private banking system known as the non-federal Federal Reserve Bank".**

Consider this fact. When an IRS agent wants to seize property from a Citizen in a County, **they must first contact the Sheriff of the County and request assistance in the seizure.** This is because the IRS agent has no authority to seize any property at all. So the IRS agent bamboozles the Sheriff into committing the crime *for the IRS.* When the Sheriff seizes property from a Citizen under the non-authority of the IRS agent, **the Sheriff has committed a Second Degree Felony; Conversion of Property.**

A second degree felony is incredibly serious. However, both the IRS agent counts on the abysmal ignorance of the Citizen who has no idea what his Lawful Rights are. Bear this point in mind, since the IRS agent has no authority to seize any property at all, then he cannot delegate or confer to the Sheriff what he himself does not have. In addition, **the Sheriff has no idea that he has engaged in a serious crime.**

Here is where the maxim applies, **"Ignorance of the law, is no excuse for violating the law."** Both the IRS agent and the Sheriff are subject to arrest and should be charged with Conversion of property, a second degree felony.

Tyranny is defined as: **Dominance through threat of punishment and violence; oppressive rule; abusive government; cruelty and injustice.**

What better definition than this fits the abusive IRS.

America is using a private credit system wherein the medium of exchange are the Federal Reserve Notes that we call "Dollars". Hence, **the so-called "Income Tax" is nothing more than a disguised "User Fee" that Americans must pay to the non-federal Federal Reserve Bank for using their private credit system.** [research **Title 12 USC**].

The legal definition of "dollar" is **"a gold or silver coin of a specific weight and with specific markings".** Thus, a Federal Reserve Note, is not and cannot, ever be a dollar. **A Note is not "money"**, see Blacks Law Dictionary. The Federal Reserve Notes currently in use are mere evidence of a debt.

The Federal Reserve Banking system is not a Federal government agency; there are no "reserves" and there is no real money. The Federal Reserve Banking system is a private cartel that has usurped the authority of the Congress to coin Money.

Federal Reserve Notes are just as worthless or just as valuable as Monopoly Money used in the game "Monopoly".

If we go to **this** Constitution for the united States of America, Article I, section 8, we find that only Congress was given the authority **"To coin money, regulate the Value thereof, and of foreign Coin, and fix the Standard of Weights and Measures"**.

This authority given to Congress by **this** Constitution for the united States of America, was not to be delegated to any private corporation for that corporation's private gain.

("...**this** Constitution **for** the United States of America." [See PREAMBLE, and ARTICLE VI, clause 3] is **not** "THE CONSTITUTION **OF** THE UNITED STATES OF AMERICA" that is currently in use today.)

The authority to coin money was usurped by the unlawful enactment of the Federal Reserve Act of 1913. The Federal Reserve Act is a "private law" **passed by only four Congressmen** <u>after the Congressional session closed</u> **in December of 1913.** Congress can pass both private laws and public laws. Congress does not have to tell the American Citizens which law is private and which law is public. We are simply led to believe that all laws are public. This is propaganda and brainwashing at its best.

This was a silent coup d' e-tat wherein the American People became the slaves of the Federal Reserve Bank. The "Killing Blow", the coup de grace [pronounced gra] was delivered upon the American People by Franklin D. Roosevelt in 1933 by removing the Gold Standard from the American economy.

Since then, no American Citizen has actually paid for anything, we have just exchanged worthless Federal Reserved Notes for more worthless Federal Reserve Notes. **All we do is lease our property** from the "STATE OF NEW MEXICO", **we lease our cars, we lease our houses, WE OWN NOTHING.**

Since 1933 **no American has owned his property in Allodium. That is why the "STATE [OF NEW MEXICO]" can take our property for just about any reason, i.e Eminent domain, failure to pay so-called "property taxes", etc.**

For anyone who has ever dealt with a debt collection agency, you know how nasty, mean and dirty they can be. Now, take that nastiness, that meanness and dirtiness and multiply it one hundred fold, there you have the attitude of the IRS.

Let's continue down the Rabbit Hole. When an American Citizen gets into a dispute with the IRS, the IRS agent will not listen to any of your pleadings, your begging's or your excuses. Everything you do or say amounts to nothing with the IRS. If you dig in your heels and refuse to pay, the IRS starts sending you threatening letters with dire consequences for your non-cooperation.

If you still refuse to pay, the IRS will file a document called a **"Notice of Federal Tax Lien"** in the local County Clerk's office. This is a very deceptive document. Keep one thing in mind a "Notice" is not the "Lien" itself. The "Lien" is a totally separate and distinct document from the "Notice". **The County Clerk, through ignorance files the "Notice of Federal Tax Lien" as if it were an actual "Lien".** These are two separate and distinct documents. **The County Clerk never requests the actual "Lien" from the IRS agent.** If they were to request this document, the IRS agent would get very irate and threaten the County Clerk for their non-cooperation. Of course, **the actual "Lien" does not exist!**

There is one more lawful requirement that the County Clerk must comply with before they can file the **"Notice of Federal Tax Lien"** or the actual **"Lien"** itself.

The Federal Lien Registration Act requires "Certification" of the "Lien" itself. This would require that the IRS agent file **an Affidavit** wherein they identify themselves, and state under Oath **that there is an actual "Lien" on file based on an actual assessment on form 23C,** against the particular American Citizen. When the County Clerk **fails to verify "Certification"** they violate the lawful requirements of the Federal Lien Registration Act.

The IRS never files the actual

"Lien" because it does not exist! An actual "Lien" must be based on a lawful assessment on form 23C. In the entire history of the IRS, the IRS has never produced a form 23C showing an individual assessment against an American Citizen.

This so-called **"Notice of Federal Tax Lien"** is an act of **"Financial Terrorism"** because once this **"Notice"** is filed, *you become a pariah, a financial outcast, you are branded as unfit, you are no longer a "good slave", you are a rebel beyond the hope of redemption.* Your slave "Credit Rating" takes a nosedive. You are practically ruined financially.

Interestingly, **Section 803** of the so-called **PATRIOT ACT** defines terrorism as *"any act intended to coerce or threaten a civilian population".* So by the very definition of "Terrorism", the IRS is the largest, meanest, dirtiest, Terrorist Organization in the entire world.

If you are still not intimidated, **the IRS will file a "Notice of Levy" with the County Clerk, and send copies to your bank(s) and employer.** The County Clerk, through ignorance, **files the "Notice of Levy" as if it were an actual "Levy".** These are two separate and distinct documents.

Again, keep in mind, **a "Notice" is not a "Levy".** On this "Notice" alone, **the bank then hands over all of your money to the IRS and you cannot even pay your bills!** Your employer garnishes your paycheck, and again, *you are the slave of the Federal Reserve Bank.* Your Bank treats the "Notice of Levy" as if it were an actual "Levy". Your employer also treats the "Notice of Levy" as if it were an actual "Levy". The bank and your employer never request an actual copy of the "Levy" itself. **Of course, the actual "Levy" does not exist!**

Both the bank and your employer fail to verify several key pieces of information in dealing with the IRS agent.

First, they fail to ask for a copy of the IRS agent's driver's license to verify that in fact they are who they say they are. So that in case, the IRS agent has to be served with legal process, they can be located. **(all IRS agents have been given instructions to never provide this information to any one asking for it. Thus, the true identity of the IRS agent is never established.)** Pretty convenient, Huh!

Second, the bank and your employer fail to request a copy of the "Pocket Commission" from the IRS agent. **Every IRS agent is assigned a "Pocket Commission".** This "Pocket Commission" identifies the IRS agent's authority as to his/her actions. The most common "Pocket Commission" is what is called **"Administrative".** This is identified with a capital **"A"** on their identity card. This means that this IRS agent can shuffle paperwork all day, **but he/she does not have any "Enforcement" authority whatsoever.**

The other "Pocket Commission" is what is called **"Enforcement".** The word "Enforcement" might convey the message that this IRS agent actually has unlimited authority to **"Enforce"** something against American Citizens. That is not the case at all. They have an extremely limited scope of authority. In fact, **they cannot enforce anything against American Citizens, without a warrant from the court.**

Both the bank and your employer fail to request a copy of the "Pocket Commission" from the IRS agent in order to establish the authority of the IRS agent. **I am fairly confident that all agents that send out notices to banks and employers have an "Administrative Pocket Commission". Thus, both your bank and your employer steal your money and send it to the Terrorist Agency known as the IRS.**

Thirdly, the bank and your employer fail to request a copy of the actual assessment on form 23C. Again, **never in the history of this country has an American Citizen been assessed an Income Tax on a form 23C.** Without this so-called assessment on this specific form, form 23C, **there is no debt.** So the bank and your employer

fail to verify this alleged debt and thus, steal your money.

Fourth, the bank and your employer fail to request of copy of the **"Abstract of Court Judgment".** This document would show that you were actually sued by the IRS and **that you had your day in court.** The Seventh Amendment of the Bill of Rights of this Constitution for the united States of America guarantees you **the Right of Trial by Jury in any controversy where the amount shall exceed twenty dollars.** Of course, you were never sued and you never had your day in court. Thus, **your Due Process of Law Rights are totally violated and again,** and you are further enslaved to the Federal Reserve Bank.

So then, we come to the end of the Rabbit Hole. **You have never owed any money to the IRS!** The IRS is simply the enforcer, the debt collector for the Federal Reserve Banking System. However, because you are using a private credit system, wherein the medium of exchange are fancy pieces of paper called Federal Reserve Notes, **you allegedly owe the Federal Reserve Bank a fraudulent "user fee".**

By way of information, the IRS does not have a bank account wherein your tax payments are deposited. **All of your tax payments are deposited into the bank account of the Federal Reserve Bank in one region or another.**

The Federal Reserve Banks and the IRS constitute the single largest sting operation, the single largest fraud and the single largest swindle in the history of the World.

In order to keep this "Alice in Wonderland" illusion going, the so-called "government" developed an entire industry to support and perpetuate this fraud. **The tax preparation industry.** Tax preparers, accountants, so-called Certified Public Accountants, self proclaimed financial gurus advising about tax loopholes, etc., etc.

All the current paycheck garnishments in the entire country could be stopped by having your employer request

the above mentioned documents, to wit:

1. A copy of the **Driver's License** of the IRS agent

2. A copy of the **"Pocket Commission"** showing the authority of the IRS agent

3. A copy of the **assessment** shown on form 23C against the American Citizen

4. A copy of the **"Abstract of Court Judgment"** that verifies that you had a trial by jury.

As the elected Sheriff of San Miguel County, New Mexico, **I will provide educational classes to the County Clerk and the employers who are currently garnishing wages and paychecks to identify areas where they may have broken the law and unwittingly stolen their employees Federal Reserve Notes and thus committed "Conversion of Property", a second degree felony.**

Furthermore, **I will work closely with the County Clerk through education and knowledge so that the Clerk can stop breaking the law and committing financial terrorism against the Citizens of San Miguel County.**

When the Citizens of San Miguel County elect me as their new Sheriff in town, **I will ban the IRS from San Miguel County, and if I catch an IRS agent within the boundaries of the county, without my permission, I will arrest them for TRESPASSING**

Posted by: Bill Messier

Private Pilot K1MNW

"AOPA Member"

Maine Republic Email Alert

No.174

". . . that I should bear witness unto the truth." — *John 18:33* // *David E. Robinson, Publisher*

"*. . . if the trumpet give an uncertain sound, who shall prepare himself for battle?*" — *I Corinthians 14:8* —   07/25/12

The Organic Act of 1871

1871, February 21: Congress Passed an "Act to Provide a Government for the District of Columbia", also known as the "Act of 1871".

With no constitutional authority to do so, Congress created a separate form of government for the District of Columbia, a ten mile square parcel of land (see, Acts of the Forty-first Congress," Section 34, Session III, chapters 61 and 62).

The act — passed when the country was weakened and financially depleted in the aftermath of the Civil War — was a strategic move by foreign bankers who were intent upon gaining a stranglehold on the coffers of America.

Congress cut a deal with the international bankers and incurred a DEBT to them because they were not about to lend money to a floundering nation without serious stipulations. So they devised a way to get their foot in the door of the United States.

The Act of 1871 formed a corporation called THE UNITED STATES.

The corporation, owned by foreign interests, moved in and shoved the original Constitution aside. With the Act of 1871, the organic Constitution was altered when the title was capitalized and the word "for" was changed to "of" in the title.

THE CONSTITUTION OF THE UNITED STATES OF AMERICA is the constitution of the incorporated UNITED STATES OF AMERICA. It operates in an economic capacity and is being used to fool the People into thinking that it governs the Republic. But it does not!

Capitalization is significant when one is referring to a legal document. This seemingly "minor" alteration has had a major impact on every subsequent generation of Americans.

What Congress did by passing the Act of 1871 was create an entirely new document, a constitution for the government of the District of Columbia, an INCORPORATED business.

This newly altered Act of 1871 Constitution was not intended to benefit the Republic. It benefits the corporation of THE UNITED STATES OF AMERICA and operates entirely outside the original organic Constitution.

Instead of having absolute and unalienable rights guaranteed under the organic Constitution, we the people now have "relative" rights, or privileges. One example is the Sovereign's right to travel, that has now been transformed (under corporate government policy) into a "privilege" that requires citizens to be licensed. (Passports)

In passing the Act of 1871 Congress committed TREASON against the People who were Sovereign under the grants and decrees of the Declaration of Independence and the organic Constitution.

The Act of 1871 became the FOUNDATION of all the treason committed by government officials ever since.

To fully understand how our rights of sovereignty were ended, you must understand the full meaning of the word sovereign: *"Chief or highest, supreme power, superior in position to all others; independent of and unlimited by others; possessing or entitled to; original and independent authority or jurisdiction."* (Webster).

In short, our government, which was created by and for us as sovereigns — *free citizens deemed to have the highest authority in the land* — was stolen from us, along with our rights. Keep in mind that, according to the original, organic

Constitution, We the People are sovereign; government is not sovereign. The Declaration of Independence says that **"government is subject to the consent of the governed"**; that's us. We're sovereigns. When did you last feel like a sovereign?

It doesn't take a rocket scientist or a constitutional historian to figure out that the U.S. Government has NOT been subject to the consent of the governed since long before you or I were born.

Rather, the governed are subject to the whim and greed of the corporation, which has stretched its tentacles beyond the ten-mile-square parcel of land known as the District of Columbia. It has invaded every state of the Republic.

However, the corporation has NO jurisdiction beyond the District of Columbia. You just think it does.

You are 'presumed' to know the law, but We the People are taught NOTHING about the law in school. We memorize obscure facts and phrases, here and there, like the Preamble, which says, *"We the People...establish this Constitution for the United States of America."* But our teachers only gloss over the Bill of Rights. Our schools, which are controlled by the corporate government, don't delve into the Constitution in depth.

The corporation was established to indoctrinate and 'dumb-down' the masses, not to teach anything of value or importance. Certainly, no one mentioned that America was "sold-out" to foreign interests, and that we were obligated to pay the debt incurred by Congress, or that we are in debt to the international bankers.

Yet, for generations, Americans have had the bulk of their earnings confiscated to pay a massive debt that they did not incur and do not owe.

There's an endless stream of things that the People aren't told. And, now that you are being told, how do you feel about being made the recipient of a debt without your knowledge or consent?

After passage of the Act of 1871 Congress set a series of subtle and overt deceptions into motion, deceptions in the form of decisions that were meant to sell us down the river. Over time, the Republic took it on the chin until it was knocked down and counted out by a technical KO [knock out].

With the surrender of the people's gold in 1933, the 'common herd' was placed under illegitimate law.

(I'll bet you weren't taught THIS in school.)

Our corporate form of government is based on Roman Civil Law and Admiralty or Maritime Law, which is also known as the "Divine Right of Kings" and the "Law of the Seas" — another fact of American history not taught in our schools.

Actually, Roman Civil Law was fully established in the colonies before our nation began, and then became managed by private international law. In other words, the government — the government created for the District of Columbia via the Act of 1871 – operates under Private International Law, not the Common Law foundation of our Constitutional Republic.

This fact has impacted all Americans in concrete ways. For instance, although Private International Law is technically only applicable within the District of Columbia, and NOT in the other states of the Union, the arms of the Corporation of THE UNITED STATES are called "departments": the Justice Department; the Treasury Department; etc. And these departments affect everyone, no matter where and in what state they live.

Each department belongs to the corporation — to THE UNITED STATES.

"Refer to any UNITED STATES CODE (USC). Note the capitalization; this is evidence of a corporation, not of a Republic. For example, In Title 28 3002 (15)(A)(B)(C), it is unequivocally stated that **the UNITED STATES is a corporation.**

Translation: the corporation is NOT a separate and distinct entity; it is not disconnected from the government; **it IS the government — your government.**

This is extremely important! I refer to it as the **"Corporate EMPIRE of the UNITED STATES"** which operates under Roman Civil Law outside the original Constitution. How do you like being ruled by a corporation?

You say you'll ask your Congress-person about this? "HA!! "

Congress is fully aware of this deception. So it's time that you, too, be aware of the deception. What this great deception means is that **the members of Congress do NOT work for us, for you and me. They work for the Corporation, for the UNITED STATES.** No wonder we can't get them to do anything on our behalf, or meet or demands, or answer our questions.

Technically, legally, or any other way you want to look at the matter, **the corporate government of the UNITED STATES has no jurisdiction or authority in ANY State of the Union (the Republic) beyond the District of Columbia.**

Let that tidbit sink in, then ask yourself, could this deception have occurred without the full knowledge and complicity of the Congress? Do you think it happened by accident? If you do, you're deceiving yourself.

There are no accidents, no coincidences. Face the facts and confront the truth. Remember, you are presumed to know the law. THEY know you don't know the law or, for that matter, your history. Why?

Because no concerted effort was ever made to teach or otherwise inform you. As a Sovereign, you are entitled to full disclosure of all facts. As a slave, you are entitled to nothing other than what the corporation decides to 'give' you.

Remember also that "Ignorance of the law is no excuse." It's your responsibility and obligation to learn the law and know how it applies to you. No wonder the Act of 1871 corporation counted on the fact that most people are too indifferent,

unconcerned, distracted, or lazy to learn what they need to know to survive within the system. We have been conditioned to let the government do our thinking for us. Now's the time to turn that around if we intend to help save our Republic and ourselves — before it's too late.

As an instrument of the international bankers, the UNITED STATES owns you from birth to death. It also holds ownership of all your assets, of your property, even of your children. Think long and hard about all the bills taxes, fines, and licenses you have paid for or purchased. Yes, they had you by the pockets.

If you don't believe it, read the 14th Amendment. See how "free" you really are. Ignorance of the facts led to your silence. **Silence is construed as consent;** consent to be obligated for a debt you did not incur. As a Sovereign People we have been deceived for hundreds of years; **we think we are free, but in truth we are servants of the corporation.**

Congress committed treason against the People in 1871. Honest men could have corrected the fraud and treason. But there weren't enough honest men to counteract the lust for money and power. We lost more freedom than we will ever know, thanks to corporate infiltration of our so-called "government".

Do you think that any soldier who died in any of our many wars would have fought if he or she had known the truth? Do you think one person would have laid down his/her life for a corporation? How long will we remain silent? How long will we perpetuate THE MYTH that we are free? When will we stand together as One Sovereign People? When will we take back what has been as stolen from the us?

If the People of America had known to what extent their trust has been betrayed, how long would it have taken for a real revolution to occur? What we now need is a Revolution in THOUGHT.

We need to change our thinking, then we can change our world. Our children deserve their rightful legacy — the liberty our ancestors fought to preserve, the legacy of a Sovereign and Fully Free People.

Maine Republic Email Alert

No.156

". . . that I should bear witness unto the truth." — John 18:33 // David E. Robinson, Publisher

". . . if the trumpet give an uncertain sound, who shall prepare himself for battle?" — I Corinthians 14:8 — 07/081/12

Maine Governor Paul LePage Speaks Out !

Gov. LePage calls IRS "new Gestapo" in his weekly radio address!

During his weekly radio address, Gov. Paul LePage reacted to the US Supreme Court's decision on the Affordable Health Care Act strongly, describing President Obama's health care reform in harsh terms and referring to the IRS as the "new Gestapo."

In arguing the court's decision made America less free, LePage said, "We the people have been told there is no choice. You must buy health insurance or pay the new Gestapo - the I.R.S." The governor also said he needs more information before deciding whether to expand the state's Medicaid program, a part of the law the court struck down, but the federal government would pay all of the cost for the expansion from 2014 to 2016 before reducing its support to 90 percent of the cost.

On Saturday, Maine Governor Paul LePage called the IRS the "new Gestapo" in his weekly radio address, the Portland Free Press reported.

"We the people have been told there is no choice," the Maine Republican said. "You must buy health insurance or pay the new Gestapo – the IRS."

Gov. LePage was referring to a provision in the health care law recently upheld by the Supreme Court that says Americans must either buy health insurance or face a stiff penalty. That provision, known as the individual mandate, is to be enforced by the Internal Revenue Service.

According to the Governor, the court

decision has "made America less free," and gives the government too much control over individual's lives.

According to the Governor, the court decision has "made America less free," and gives the government too much control over individual's lives.

"Perhaps what is most disturbing about this ruling, though, is that the federal mandate is considered a tax," he said. *"This tax will add to the $500 billion in tax increases that are already in Obamacare. Now that Congress can use the taxation power of the federal government to com*

A 2010 report at the Washington Examiner said the new taxes and mandates "will cause the greatest

expansion of the Internal Revenue Service since World War II," with an estimated 16,500 new agents.

Maine Democrats did not care for Gov. LePage's characterization.

The Press Herald added:

Maine Democratic Party Chairman Ben Grant, responding to LePage's remarks, said, *"We've come to expect a bunch of nonsense from Gov. LePage, but this is a step too far. There appears now to be no limit to the extreme language he will use to misinform, degrade and insult people. Somebody needs to explain to him that he's the governor of a state, and not a talk radio host. I demand a full apology on behalf of all those who suffered at the hands of the real Gestapo."*

The feared Gestapo was the official secret police in Hitler's Germany, and was responsible for the deaths of thousands in the Third Reich.

Gov. LePage also said the state would not move forward on the healthcare exchanges, due to "looming uncertainties" over funding.

President Obama, he said, "has proposed $800 million to finance exchanges," but that money has not been approved by Congress.

"Government-run health care is not what the American dream is about," he added.

"America wasn't born on these sorts of principles and it's time we get back on track - not only for our future generations, but for the future of our Nation," he concluded.

"ad Christi potentium et gloriam"
(for the power and glory of Christ)

Maine Republic Email Alert   *No.157*

". . . that I should bear witness unto the truth." — John 18:33 // David E. Robinson, Publisher

". . . if the trumpet give an uncertain sound, who shall prepare himself for battle?" — I Corinthians 14:8 —   07/091/12

Request For Discovery !

DAVID E. ROBINSON, ELECTED ATTORNEY GENERAL FOR THE MAINE FREE STATE TRUST

3 Linnell Circle, Brunswick, Maine 04011

May 16, 2012

This **"Request for Discovery"** is in regard to the fraudulent IRS NOTICES OF LIEN being sent to you — Accounts Payable — by the IRS against F. WILLIAM MESSIER, 40 Tower Lane, Brunswick ME 04011.

DEAR ACCOUNTS PAYABLE,

The Federal Reserve is no more a federal agency than is Federal Express!

The Internal Revenue Service is no more a federal agency than is Dagget & Parker, or McDonalds!

The "Internal Revenue Service" is incorporated in Delaware as a "collection agency" for a Puerto Rican Company titled "Internal Revenue Tax & Audit Service" (IRS) — a for-profit corporation — Incorporated on 07/12/33 — File No. 0325720.

Therefore the "Internal Revenue Service" must be recognized in its lawful status as a "DEBT COLLECTION AGENCY" [under Title 15 instead of Title 26] and not be fraudulently accepted as a [U.S.] "Government Agency".

A "Notice of Levy" is not a "Levy"! — In dealing with an IRS "debt collector" Agent (or any other "debt collector") the following Seven items of information need to be obtained for "Proof of Claim".

(1) Ask the IRS Agent for a copy of his "DRIVER'S LICENSE" to verify that he is who he says he is. You need to record the "License Number" for possible use in case he has to be served with legal papers, so he can be located for proper service.

Gov. LePage calls IRS "new Gestapo" in his weekly radio address!

During his weekly radio address, Gov. Paul LePage reacted to the US Supreme Court's decision on the Affordable Health Care Act strongly, describing President Obama's health care reform in harsh terms and referring to the IRS as the "new Gestapo." In arguing the court's decision made America less free, LePage said, "We the people have been told there is no choice. You must buy health insurance or pay the new Gestapo - the I.R.S." The governor also said he needs more information before deciding whether to expand the state's Medicaid program, a part of the law the court struck down, but the federal government would pay all of the cost for the expansion from 2014 to 2016 before reducing its support to 90 percent of the cost.

(2) Ask the IRS Agent for a copy of his "POCKET COMMISSION MANUAL" showing his "authority to act" in this case. The most common type is "Administrator" (type A). The second type is "Enforcer" (type E). Administrators can only shuffle the paperwork. They cannot enforce the IRS law.

(3) Ask the IRS Agent for a copy of the "ACTUAL ASSESSMENT" — NOT the 668-A Notice of Levy — showing what the IRS claims the alleged "taxpayer" owes — according to the Internal Revenue, that the Internal Revenue Service is authorized to collect.

(4) Ask the IRS Agent for a copy of the "ABSTRACT OF COURT JUDGMENT" that verifies that the alleged "taxpayer" has a Jury Trial before any of his assets could be seized.

(5) Demand that the IRS Agent confirm all of his written answers under the penalty of perjury.

(6) Demand that the IRS Agent provide you with a copy of the "missing part (a)" (of Section 6331 "Levy and Distraint") missing on the back of the 668-A "Notice of Levy".

(7) Ask the IRS Agent which "Title" he is operating under — Title 26 of the "IR Code" or Title 15 of the "US Code" regarding corporations.

The Internal Revenue (IR) is a government agency under Title 26 of the "IR Code" Manual.

The Internal Revenue Service (IRS) is a private foreign for-profit "debt-collection agency" — it is not connected with any government — it operates under Title 15 of the "US Code".

By sending Mr. F. William Messier's Property (his money) to the IRS without judicial process of law and without first having verified the AUTHENTICITY of the

IRS Agent's claims, you may be liable

to PROSECUTION for having committed illegal "CONVERSION OF PROPERTY" — which is a second degree felony punishable by a fine and/or imprisonment or both.

Debt-collection agencies are subject to Title 15 of the United States Code relating to "Verified Assessment" whereby the "Debt Collection Agency" (of which you are now a debt-collector extension) must provide "proof of the claim" to validate the debt.

Any case involving the collection of debt must have been adjudicated in a local judicial district court.

The IRS has no way to verify an alleged debt without the alleged "taxpayer" voluntarily assessing himself.

According to Title 15, Section 1692, a debt-collector...

1. must legally identify himself;

2. must not state that the consumer owes any debt;

3. must not use any symbol that indicates that he is in the debt-collection business;

4. must not imply that he is affiliated with the United States Government or any of the states.

It is obvious that the IRS Agent has NOT obeyed these legal requirements in this case.

Please acknowledge the receipt of this letter by sending an email from a company contact to:

F. William Messier-- k1mnw@yahoo.com

David E. Robinson -- drobin88@comcast.net

Obtain Copies of the (7) Items of Verification listed above from IRS "DEBT-COLLECTION AGENT" JOLINE P. HENDERSHOT, 217 MAIN STREET, LEWISTON ME 04240, and from IRS "DEBT-COLLECTION AGENT" PATRICK FRIE, 220 MAINE MALL ROAD, SOUTH PORTLAND ME 04106.

Send duplicate copies, and copies of all correspondence sent to you from the IRS, to me by snail mail, to the above letterhead-address, within the next twenty (20) days from your receipt of this Demand. More time will be granted upon your written request. Failure to timely comply will be taken as material evidence that you refuse to honor this Demand.

I await your timely response.

Sincerely,

David E. Robinson
Interim Attorney General
for the Maine Free State Trust

Attached:

Maine Republic Email Newsletter Alerts:

#087 The Internal Revenue is not the Internal Revenue Service

#088 Nil-dicit Judgment ("he says nothing" judgment)

#090 IRS Levis and Liens

#094 IRS Strategy

#095 Internal Revenue Service Personnel

- X - X - X - X - X - X - X- X - X - X - X - X - X - X- X - X - X - X - X - X - X - X - X - X - X - X - X - X - X - X - X - X - X -

DISCLAIMER

Please note that the court system in America is an adversarial dual between a challenged party and a respondent party adversarially fought with ideas, concepts, and words instead of with the weapons of war, therefore in this report, names have not been removed to protect those who are alleged to be guilty. In this New World Order of intimate surveillance that we have naively allowed to take place the "third eye" above the pyramid of illuminati power is ever watching the sovereign people of America for the evil purpose of keeping all Americans dumbed down and enslaved. Note that AS MAINE GOES SO GOES THE NATION!

http://americannationalmilitia.com/
http://americannationalmilitia.com/2012/07/notice-to-the-world-was-delivered-to-the-office-of-private-international-law-at-the-hague/
http://americannationalmilitia.com/wp-content/uploads/2012/07/148-NOTICE-to-the-world.pdf

Layers of Conspiracy

By Cobra:

At the core of the physical Cabal there is a group of 13 Archons that has been controlling our planet for the last 26,000 years. They are responsible for the fall of Atlantis, for the collapse of peaceful Goddess worshipping neolithic cultures 5000 years ago, and for the destruction of the mystery schools in late antiquity. They are the ones that maintained the quarantine and kept humanity hostage so that the positive ETs could not intervene until now. They are mostly incarnated into key positions inside the Italian black nobility.

Their leader was arrested in Rome on May 5th, 2012, removed from this planet, and taken immediately to the Galactic Central Sun. He was the one that many members of the Cabal were worshipping in their distorted rituals, so now they are worshipping something that does not exist any longer.

About 2500 years ago, the Archons created a special task group and infiltrated it into the Ptolemaic dynasty in Egypt:

http://tinyurl.com/cc4hb72

This task group was responsible for the mind programming and mass control of humanity through organized religions during the last 2500 years. After the death of Cleopatra, their power was transferred from the Ptolemaic bloodline towards the Julio-Claudean dynasty in Rome, then to the Flavians, then to the Constantinian dynasty, then to the Theodosian dynasty and then to the Byzantine Giustiniani family. After the middle ages, members of this group incarnated mostly into positions of power within the Italian black nobility families. The Resistance took strong actions against this group in 2010 and it lost much of its power then.

This group created the Jesuits and the Jesuits have been running the show on this planet for the last 500 years, as you can read in this fairly accurate, although somewhat outdated report:

http://www.whale.to/b/pope.html

http://tinyurl.com/cf7e43a

Hans Kolvenbach is the old black Pope, the new one is Adolfo Nicolas.

This is how the Jesuits run the USA corporation:

http://tinyurl.com/cr3puwx

The Rothschilds have been the bankers for the Jesuits during the last two centuries. The most influential are: Jacob de Rothschild, Evelyn de Rothschild, David de Rothschild and lately also Nathaniel Philip de Rothschild.

The Rockefeller-Illuminazi faction is a Jesuit creation of the 20th century with a purpose to hinder and misuse the technological and scientific progress of humanity:

http://tinyurl.com/cbum6tj

The key players of the Rockefeller-Illuminazi faction are: David Rockefeller, Henry Kissinger, George Herbert Walker Bush (George Scherf Jr.), Dick Cheney, Jay Rockefeller, Donald Rumsfeld, Karl Rove and Paul Wolfowitz.

"ad Christi potentium et gloriam"
(for the power and glory of Christ)

The Maine Republic Free State Trust

02-10-2012

A Trust is a three party contract between a Beneficiary, an Executor, and a Trustee.

A Trust is a three party contract based on the Trinity of the Bible — the Father; the Son; and the Holy Ghost.

The Bible is God's Last Will & Testament. A Testament is testimony left by a Testator in a Will.

The Father is the Testator, the Son is the Beneficiary, and the Holy Spirit provides the Energy and the Will to perform.

A good way to understand Trusts is to think of Corporations, because a trust is a corporation under different terms.

A Corporation has Shareholders, Directors, and Employees.

A Trust has Beneficiaries, Executors, and Trustees.

The Trustees hold and manage the property for the benefit of the Beneficiaries, as instructed by the Executor according to the terms of the trust agreement.

Trustees obey the Executor, for the benefit of the Beneficiaries;

Just as Employees obey the Director, for the benefit of the Shareholders;

Just as the Spirit must be in line with the Father's Will, for the benefit of the Son.

A Trustee can't be the Executor or a Beneficiary of a trust; just as an Employee can't be the Director or a Shareholder of a corporation... and visa, versa.

An Executor or a Beneficiary can't be a Trustee; just as a Director or a Shareholder can't be an Employee.

What the Great Testator gave us to enjoy, develope, and maintain, is held in trust for us by our government employees.

In the trust called the **Maine Free State**, the Executor/Governor was John V.; the Beneficiaries/Members were the citizens of the state; and the Officers/Trustees were the officials of the trust.

On the basis of the Maxim *"Until it is documented, it doesn't exist"* — *and in behalf of the citizens of the state* — the Attorny General documented **The Maine Republic Free State** as a trust, by donating the equity in his Mobile Home to the Trust, as the Corpus or body of the trust, for the benefit of the citizens of the state, each having an equal share.

The trust called The United States Corporation

Compare the above with the U.S. Corporation, *which is also a trust,* which has been perverted in its execution, by the state.

The government employees are the Trustees who hold the public property of the Trust for the benefit of the Executor (the Corp) and themselves. They reversed the roles of the trust whereby the Beneficiaries are treated as Trustees instead of the Beneficiaries that they are.

You are a *natural* person as defined in Black's Law dictionary.

Your strawman is an *artificial* person established by law — as a corporation, or trust.

There are only two kinds of law. God's law, and man's law. Natural law, and Contract law. The *lawful* person, and the legal person. The *natural* person, and the *artificial* person.

But, in the U.S. Corporation government officials tell the citizens what to do, for the benefit of government employees, and the state.

Whereas, in a Republic, citiizens tell the government employees what to do, for the benefit of themselves as citizens, and the state.

In the U.S. Corporation, citizens of the state are treated a government employees, of the state — by presumption — not by fact.

And the *Strawman* is the Bait for the "Bait and Switch."

Your legal name is a *presumption of law.* They have to get you to join into their law, and act as an employee, instead of the citizen that you are — to act as a trustee, instead of the beneficiary that you are — to take orders from the state, instead of directing the state to obey the Constitution as the "Law of the Land" that it is.

Who is the Beneficiary of your estate? You are!

Who is the Executor of your estate? You are!

Who are the Trustees of your estate? Government employees!

The government and the courts operate on presumption. They deal in presumptions that until rebutted stand as law.

So, rebut the presumptions by rebutting the contracts that don't exist. Anything *after* Man is a legal contract; a fiction.

So, ask yourself this: Where is the contract? What obligation does the contract claim? Was I aware of the contract? Did I agree to the contract? Where is the consideration? Was the contract fully disclosed?

Don't be conned into being the Trustee. Be the *Administrator/Executor/Director* of your estate. A Director directs; Trustees obey.

Complaint and Motion for Summary Judgement or Jury Trial

DAVID E. ROBINSON, INTERIM ATTORNEY GENERAL FOR THE MAINE FREE STATE
3 LINNELL CIRCLE, BRUNSWICK, MAINE 04011

May 16, 2012

This "**Request for Discovery**" is in regard to the fraudulent IRS **NOTICES OF LIEN** being sent to you by the IRS against **F. WILLIAM MESSIER**, 40 Tower Lane, Brunswick ME 04011.

DEAR ACCOUNTS PAYABLE,

The Federal Reserve is no more a federal agency than is **Federal Express!**
The Internal Revenue Service in no more a federal agency than is **Dagget & Parker, or McDonalds!**

The "**Internal Revenue Service**" is incorporated in Delaware as a "collection agency" for a Puerto Rican Company titled "Internal Revenue Tax & Audit Service" (IRS) — a for-profit corporation — Incorporated on 07/12/33 — File No. 0325720.

Therefore the "**Internal Revenue Service**" must be recognized in its lawful status as a "**DEBT COLLECTION AGENCY**" and not be fraudulently accepted as a "**Government Agency**".

A "**Notice of Levy**" is not a "**Levy**"! — In dealing with an **IRS "debt collector" Agent (or any other "debt collector")** the following **Seven items** of information need to be obtained for "**Proof of Claim**".

(1) **Ask** the IRS Agent for a copy of his "**DRIVER'S LICENSE**" to verify that he is who he says he is. You need to record the "**License Number**" for possible use in case he has to be served with legal papers, so he can be located for proper service.

(2) **Ask** the IRS Agent for a copy of his "**POCKET COMMISSION MANUAL**" showing his "authority to act" in this case. The most common type is "**Administrator**" (**type A**). The second type is "**Enforcer**" (**type E**). Administrators can only shuffle the paperwork. They cannot enforce the IRS law.

(3) **Ask** the IRS Agent for a copy of the "**ACTUAL ASSESSMENT**" — **NOT the 668-A Notice of Levy** — showing what the IRS claims the alleged "taxpayer" owes — according to the **Internal Revenue**, that the **Internal Revenue Service** is authorized to collect.

(4) **Ask** the IRS Agent for a copy of the "**ABSTRACT OF COURT JUDGMENT**" that verifies that the alleged "taxpayer" has a **Jury Trial** before any of his assets could be seized.

(5) **Demand** that the IRS Agent **confirm all of his written answers under the penalty of perjury.**

(6) **Demand** that the IRS Agent **provide you with a copy of the "missing part (a)" (of Section 6331 "Levy and Distraint") missing on the back of the 668-A "Notice of Levy".**

(7) **Ask** the IRS Agent which "**Title**" he is operating under — **Title 26 of the "IR Code"** or **Title 15 of the "US Code"** regarding corporations.

The Internal Revenue (IR) is a government agency under **Title 26 of the "IR Code" Manual.**

The Internal Revenue Service (IRS) is a **private foreign for-profit "debt-collection agency"** — **it is not connected with any government** — it operates under **Title 15 of the "US Code".**

By sending **Mr. F. William Messier's Property (his money)** to the IRS **without judicial process of law** and **without first having verified the AUTHENTICITY of the IRS Agent's claims,** you may be liable to **PROSECUTION** for having committed illegal **"CONVERSION OF PROPERTY"** — **which is a second degree felony punishable by a fine and/or imprisonment or both.**

Debt-collection agencies are subject to **Title 15 of the United States Code** relating to **"Verified Assessment"** whereby the **"Debt Collection Agency" (of which you are now a debt-collector extension)** must provide **"proof of the claim"** to validate the debt.

Any case involving the collection of debt must have been adjudicated in a local judicial district court.

The IRS has no way to verify an alleged debt without the alleged "taxpayer" voluntarily assessing himself.

According to **Title 15, Section 1692,** a debt-collector...
1. **must legally identify himself;**
2. **must not state that the consumer owes any debt;**
3. **must not use any symbol that indicates that he is in the debt-collection business;**
4. **must not imply that he is affiliated with the United States Government or any of the states.**

It is obvious that the IRS Agent has NOT obeyed these legal requirements in this case.

Please acknowledge the receipt of this letter by sending an email from a company contact to:
      F. William Messier <k1mnw@yahoo.com>
      David E. Robinson <drobin88@comcast.net>

Obtain Copies of the **(7) Items of Verification** listed above from IRS "DEBT-COLLECTION AGENT" **JOLINE P. HENDERSHOT**, 217 MAIN STREET, LEWISTON ME 04240, and from IRS "DEBT-COLLECTION AGENT" **PATRICK FRIE**, 220 MAINE MALL ROAD, SOUTH PORTLAND ME 04106 **and send duplicate copies, and copies of all correspondence sent to you from the IRS, to me by snail mail, to the above letterhead-address, within the next twenty (20) days from your receipt of this Demand.** More time will be granted upon your written request. **Failure to timely comply will be taken as material evidence that you refuse to honor this Demand.**

I await your timely response.

                                    Sincerely,

                                    David E. Robinson
                                    Interim Attorney General for the Maine Free State

Attached:

Maine Republic Email Newsletter Alerts:
      087 The Internal Revenue is not the Internal Revenue Service
      088 Nil-dicit Judgment ("he says nothing" judgment)
      090 IRS Levis and Liens
      094 IRS Strategy
      095 Internal Revenue Service Personnel

AS MAINE GOES . . .
SO GOES THE NATION !

Made in United States
Orlando, FL
27 April 2022